ISBN 0-8373-4083-7
C-4083   CAREER EXAMINATION SE

This is your
PASSBOOK® for...

Street Maintenance Supervisor

Test Preparation Study Guide
Questions & Answers

NATIONAL LEARNING CORPORATION

PASSBOOK® SERIES

THE *PASSBOOK® SERIES* has been created to prepare applicants and candidates for the ultimate academic battlefield – the examination room.

At some time in our lives, each and every one of us may be required to take an examination – for validation, matriculation, admission, qualification, registration, certification, or licensure.

Based on the assumption that every applicant or candidate has met the basic formal educational standards, has taken the required number of courses, and read the necessary texts, the *PASSBOOK® SERIES* furnishes the one special preparation which may assure passing with confidence, instead of failing with insecurity. Examination questions – together with answers – are furnished as the basic vehicle for study so that the mysteries of the examination and its compounding difficulties may be eliminated or diminished by a sure method.

This book is meant to help you pass your examination provided that you qualify and are serious in your objective.

The entire field is reviewed through the huge store of content information which is succinctly presented through a provocative and challenging approach – the question-and-answer method.

A climate of success is established by furnishing the correct answers at the end of each test.

You soon learn to recognize types of questions, forms of questions, and patterns of questioning. You may even begin to anticipate expected outcomes.

You perceive that many questions are repeated or adapted so that you can gain acute insights, which may enable you to score many sure points.

You learn how to confront new questions, or types of questions, and to attack them confidently and work out the correct answers.

You note objectives and emphases, and recognize pitfalls and dangers, so that you may make positive educational adjustments.

Moreover, you are kept fully informed in relation to new concepts, methods, practices, and directions in the field.

You discover that you are actually taking the examination all the time: you are preparing for the examination by "taking" an examination, not by reading extraneous and/or supererogatory textbooks.

In short, this PASSBOOK®, used directedly, should be an important factor in helping you to pass your test.

STREET MAINTENANCE SUPERVISOR

DUTIES
This position exists in the Department of Public Works and involves responsibility for the efficient and economical use of personnel, materials and equipment in a variety of street/public works construction and maintenance activities. The work is carried out in accordance with established policies and procedures under the general supervision of the Commissioner of Public Works or other supervisor with leeway permitted in carrying out details of the work. The work is reviewed by on-site inspections and through progress reports. Supervision is exercised over the activities of subordinate equipment operators and laborers assigned to specific public works projects. The incumbent does related work as required.

SCOPE OF THE EXAMINATION
The <u>written test</u> will cover knowledge, skills and/or abilities in such areas as:

1. Methods and materials of road reconstruction;
2. Maintenance and reconstruction of streets, sidewalks and curbs;
3. Safety practices;
4. Plans, specifications and technical instructions; and
5. Supervision.

HOW TO TAKE A TEST

I. YOU MUST PASS AN EXAMINATION

A. WHAT EVERY CANDIDATE SHOULD KNOW

Examination applicants often ask us for help in preparing for the written test. What can I study in advance? What kinds of questions will be asked? How will the test be given? How will the papers be graded?

As an applicant for a civil service examination, you may be wondering about some of these things. Our purpose here is to suggest effective methods of advance study and to describe civil service examinations.

Your chances for success on this examination can be increased if you know how to prepare. Those "pre-examination jitters" can be reduced if you know what to expect. You can even experience an adventure in good citizenship if you know why civil service exams are given.

B. WHY ARE CIVIL SERVICE EXAMINATIONS GIVEN?

Civil service examinations are important to you in two ways. As a citizen, you want public jobs filled by employees who know how to do their work. As a job seeker, you want a fair chance to compete for that job on an equal footing with other candidates. The best-known means of accomplishing this two-fold goal is the competitive examination.

Exams are widely publicized throughout the nation. They may be administered for jobs in federal, state, city, municipal, town or village governments or agencies.

Any citizen may apply, with some limitations, such as the age or residence of applicants. Your experience and education may be reviewed to see whether you meet the requirements for the particular examination. When these requirements exist, they are reasonable and applied consistently to all applicants. Thus, a competitive examination may cause you some uneasiness now, but it is your privilege and safeguard.

C. HOW ARE CIVIL SERVICE EXAMS DEVELOPED?

Examinations are carefully written by trained technicians who are specialists in the field known as "psychological measurement," in consultation with recognized authorities in the field of work that the test will cover. These experts recommend the subject matter areas or skills to be tested; only those knowledges or skills important to your success on the job are included. The most reliable books and source materials available are used as references. Together, the experts and technicians judge the difficulty level of the questions.

Test technicians know how to phrase questions so that the problem is clearly stated. Their ethics do not permit "trick" or "catch" questions. Questions may have been tried out on sample groups, or subjected to statistical analysis, to determine their usefulness.

Written tests are often used in combination with performance tests, ratings of training and experience, and oral interviews. All of these measures combine to form the best-known means of finding the right person for the right job.

II. HOW TO PASS THE WRITTEN TEST

A. NATURE OF THE EXAMINATION

To prepare intelligently for civil service examinations, you should know how they differ from school examinations you have taken. In school you were assigned certain definite pages to read or subjects to cover. The examination questions were quite detailed and usually emphasized memory. Civil service exams, on the other hand, try to discover your present ability to perform the duties of a position, plus your potentiality to learn these duties. In other words, a civil service exam attempts to predict how successful you will be. Questions cover such a broad area that they cannot be as minute and detailed as school exam questions.

In the public service similar kinds of work, or positions, are grouped together in one "class." This process is known as *position-classification*. All the positions in a class are paid according to the salary range for that class. One class title covers all of these positions, and they are all tested by the same examination.

B. FOUR BASIC STEPS

1) Study the announcement

How, then, can you know what subjects to study? Our best answer is: "Learn as much as possible about the class of positions for which you've applied." The exam will test the knowledge, skills and abilities needed to do the work.

Your most valuable source of information about the position you want is the official exam announcement. This announcement lists the training and experience qualifications. Check these standards and apply only if you come reasonably close to meeting them.

The brief description of the position in the examination announcement offers some clues to the subjects which will be tested. Think about the job itself. Review the duties in your mind. Can you perform them, or are there some in which you are rusty? Fill in the blank spots in your preparation.

Many jurisdictions preview the written test in the exam announcement by including a section called "Knowledge and Abilities Required," "Scope of the Examination," or some similar heading. Here you will find out specifically what fields will be tested.

2) Review your own background

Once you learn in general what the position is all about, and what you need to know to do the work, ask yourself which subjects you already know fairly well and which need improvement. You may wonder whether to concentrate on improving your strong areas or on building some background in your fields of weakness. When the announcement has specified "some knowledge" or "considerable knowledge," or has used adjectives like "beginning principles of…" or "advanced … methods," you can get a clue as to the number and difficulty of questions to be asked in any given field. More questions, and hence broader coverage, would be included for those subjects which are more important in the work. Now weigh your strengths and weaknesses against the job requirements and prepare accordingly.

3) Determine the level of the position

Another way to tell how intensively you should prepare is to understand the level of the job for which you are applying. Is it the entering level? In other words, is this the position in which beginners in a field of work are hired? Or is it an intermediate or advanced level? Sometimes this is indicated by such words as "Junior" or "Senior" in the class title. Other jurisdictions use Roman numerals to designate the level – Clerk I, Clerk II, for example. The word "Supervisor" sometimes appears in the title. If the level is not indicated by the title, check the description of duties. Will you be working under very close supervision, or will you have responsibility for independent decisions in this work?

4) Choose appropriate study materials

Now that you know the subjects to be examined and the relative amount of each subject to be covered, you can choose suitable study materials. For beginning level jobs, or even advanced ones, if you have a pronounced weakness in some aspect of your training, read a modern, standard textbook in that field. Be sure it is up to date and has general coverage. Such books are normally available at your library, and the librarian will be glad to help you locate one. For entry-level positions, questions of appropriate difficulty are chosen – neither highly advanced questions, nor those too simple. Such questions require careful thought but not advanced training.

If the position for which you are applying is technical or advanced, you will read more advanced, specialized material. If you are already familiar with the basic principles of your field, elementary textbooks would waste your time. Concentrate on advanced textbooks and technical periodicals. Think through the concepts and review difficult problems in your field.

These are all general sources. You can get more ideas on your own initiative, following these leads. For example, training manuals and publications of the government agency which employs workers in your field can be useful, particularly for technical and professional positions. A letter or visit to the government department involved may result in more specific study suggestions, and certainly will provide you with a more definite idea of the exact nature of the position you are seeking.

III. KINDS OF TESTS

Tests are used for purposes other than measuring knowledge and ability to perform specified duties. For some positions, it is equally important to test ability to make adjustments to new situations or to profit from training. In others, basic mental abilities not dependent on information are essential. Questions which test these things may not appear as pertinent to the duties of the position as those which test for knowledge and information. Yet they are often highly important parts of a fair examination. For very general questions, it is almost impossible to help you direct your study efforts. What we can do is to point out some of the more common of these general abilities needed in public service positions and describe some typical questions.

1) General information

Broad, general information has been found useful for predicting job success in some kinds of work. This is tested in a variety of ways, from vocabulary lists to questions about current events. Basic background in some field of work, such as sociology or economics, may be sampled in a group of questions. Often these are principles which have become familiar to most persons through exposure rather than through formal training. It is difficult to advise you how to study for these questions; being alert to the world around you is our best suggestion.

2) Verbal ability

An example of an ability needed in many positions is verbal or language ability. Verbal ability is, in brief, the ability to use and understand words. Vocabulary and grammar tests are typical measures of this ability. Reading comprehension or paragraph interpretation questions are common in many kinds of civil service tests. You are given a paragraph of written material and asked to find its central meaning.

3) Numerical ability

Number skills can be tested by the familiar arithmetic problem, by checking paired lists of numbers to see which are alike and which are different, or by interpreting charts and graphs. In the latter test, a graph may be printed in the test booklet which you are asked to use as the basis for answering questions.

4) Observation

A popular test for law-enforcement positions is the observation test. A picture is shown to you for several minutes, then taken away. Questions about the picture test your ability to observe both details and larger elements.

5) Following directions

In many positions in the public service, the employee must be able to carry out written instructions dependably and accurately. You may be given a chart with several columns, each column listing a variety of information. The questions require you to carry out directions involving the information given in the chart.

6) Skills and aptitudes

Performance tests effectively measure some manual skills and aptitudes. When the skill is one in which you are trained, such as typing or shorthand, you can practice. These tests are often very much like those given in business school or high school courses. For many of the other skills and aptitudes, however, no short-time preparation can be made. Skills and abilities natural to you or that you have developed throughout your lifetime are being tested.

Many of the general questions just described provide all the data needed to answer the questions and ask you to use your reasoning ability to find the answers. Your best preparation for these tests, as well as for tests of facts and ideas, is to be at your physical and mental best. You, no doubt, have your own methods of getting into an exam-taking mood and keeping "in shape." The next section lists some ideas on this subject.

IV. KINDS OF QUESTIONS

Only rarely is the "essay" question, which you answer in narrative form, used in civil service tests. Civil service tests are usually of the short-answer type. Full instructions for answering these questions will be given to you at the examination. But in case this is your first experience with short-answer questions and separate answer sheets, here is what you need to know:

1) Multiple-choice Questions

Most popular of the short-answer questions is the "multiple choice" or "best answer" question. It can be used, for example, to test for factual knowledge, ability to solve problems or judgment in meeting situations found at work.

A multiple-choice question is normally one of three types—
- It can begin with an incomplete statement followed by several possible endings. You are to find the one ending which *best* completes the statement, although some of the others may not be entirely wrong.
- It can also be a complete statement in the form of a question which is answered by choosing one of the statements listed.

- It can be in the form of a problem – again you select the best answer.

Here is an example of a multiple-choice question with a discussion which should give you some clues as to the method for choosing the right answer:

When an employee has a complaint about his assignment, the action which will *best* help him overcome his difficulty is to
- A. discuss his difficulty with his coworkers
- B. take the problem to the head of the organization
- C. take the problem to the person who gave him the assignment
- D. say nothing to anyone about his complaint

In answering this question, you should study each of the choices to find which is best. Consider choice "A" – Certainly an employee may discuss his complaint with fellow employees, but no change or improvement can result, and the complaint remains unresolved. Choice "B" is a poor choice since the head of the organization probably does not know what assignment you have been given, and taking your problem to him is known as "going over the head" of the supervisor. The supervisor, or person who made the assignment, is the person who can clarify it or correct any injustice. Choice "C" is, therefore, correct. To say nothing, as in choice "D," is unwise. Supervisors have and interest in knowing the problems employees are facing, and the employee is seeking a solution to his problem.

2) True/False Questions

The "true/false" or "right/wrong" form of question is sometimes used. Here a complete statement is given. Your job is to decide whether the statement is right or wrong.

SAMPLE: A roaming cell-phone call to a nearby city costs less than a non-roaming call to a distant city.

This statement is wrong, or false, since roaming calls are more expensive.

This is not a complete list of all possible question forms, although most of the others are variations of these common types. You will always get complete directions for answering questions. Be sure you understand *how* to mark your answers – ask questions until you do.

V. RECORDING YOUR ANSWERS

Computer terminals are used more and more today for many different kinds of exams.

For an examination with very few applicants, you may be told to record your answers in the test booklet itself. Separate answer sheets are much more common. If this separate answer sheet is to be scored by machine – and this is often the case – it is highly important that you mark your answers correctly in order to get credit.

An electronic scoring machine is often used in civil service offices because of the speed with which papers can be scored. Machine-scored answer sheets must be marked with a pencil, which will be given to you. This pencil has a high graphite content which responds to the electronic scoring machine. As a matter of fact, stray dots may register as answers, so do not let your pencil rest on the answer sheet while you are pondering the correct answer. Also, if your pencil lead breaks or is otherwise defective, ask for another.

Since the answer sheet will be dropped in a slot in the scoring machine, be careful not to bend the corners or get the paper crumpled.

The answer sheet normally has five vertical columns of numbers, with 30 numbers to a column. These numbers correspond to the question numbers in your test booklet. After each number, going across the page are four or five pairs of dotted lines. These short dotted lines have small letters or numbers above them. The first two pairs may also have a "T" or "F" above the letters. This indicates that the first two pairs only are to be used if the questions are of the true-false type. If the questions are multiple choice, disregard the "T" and "F" and pay attention only to the small letters or numbers.

Answer your questions in the manner of the sample that follows:

32. The largest city in the United States is
   A. Washington, D.C.
   B. New York City
   C. Chicago
   D. Detroit
   E. San Francisco

1) Choose the answer you think is best. (New York City is the largest, so "B" is correct.)
2) Find the row of dotted lines numbered the same as the question you are answering. (Find row number 32)
3) Find the pair of dotted lines corresponding to the answer. (Find the pair of lines under the mark "B.")
4) Make a solid black mark between the dotted lines.

VI. BEFORE THE TEST

Common sense will help you find procedures to follow to get ready for an examination. Too many of us, however, overlook these sensible measures. Indeed, nervousness and fatigue have been found to be the most serious reasons why applicants fail to do their best on civil service tests. Here is a list of reminders:

- Begin your preparation early – Don't wait until the last minute to go scurrying around for books and materials or to find out what the position is all about.
- Prepare continuously – An hour a night for a week is better than an all-night cram session. This has been definitely established. What is more, a night a week for a month will return better dividends than crowding your study into a shorter period of time.
- Locate the place of the exam – You have been sent a notice telling you when and where to report for the examination. If the location is in a different town or otherwise unfamiliar to you, it would be well to inquire the best route and learn something about the building.
- Relax the night before the test – Allow your mind to rest. Do not study at all that night. Plan some mild recreation or diversion; then go to bed early and get a good night's sleep.
- Get up early enough to make a leisurely trip to the place for the test – This way unforeseen events, traffic snarls, unfamiliar buildings, etc. will not upset you.
- Dress comfortably – A written test is not a fashion show. You will be known by number and not by name, so wear something comfortable.

- Leave excess paraphernalia at home – Shopping bags and odd bundles will get in your way. You need bring only the items mentioned in the official notice you received; usually everything you need is provided. Do not bring reference books to the exam. They will only confuse those last minutes and be taken away from you when in the test room.
- Arrive somewhat ahead of time – If because of transportation schedules you must get there very early, bring a newspaper or magazine to take your mind off yourself while waiting.
- Locate the examination room – When you have found the proper room, you will be directed to the seat or part of the room where you will sit. Sometimes you are given a sheet of instructions to read while you are waiting. Do not fill out any forms until you are told to do so; just read them and be prepared.
- Relax and prepare to listen to the instructions
- If you have any physical problem that may keep you from doing your best, be sure to tell the test administrator. If you are sick or in poor health, you really cannot do your best on the exam. You can come back and take the test some other time.

VII. AT THE TEST

The day of the test is here and you have the test booklet in your hand. The temptation to get going is very strong. Caution! There is more to success than knowing the right answers. You must know how to identify your papers and understand variations in the type of short-answer question used in this particular examination. Follow these suggestions for maximum results from your efforts:

1) Cooperate with the monitor
The test administrator has a duty to create a situation in which you can be as much at ease as possible. He will give instructions, tell you when to begin, check to see that you are marking your answer sheet correctly, and so on. He is not there to guard you, although he will see that your competitors do not take unfair advantage. He wants to help you do your best.

2) Listen to all instructions
Don't jump the gun! Wait until you understand all directions. In most civil service tests you get more time than you need to answer the questions. So don't be in a hurry. Read each word of instructions until you clearly understand the meaning. Study the examples, listen to all announcements and follow directions. Ask questions if you do not understand what to do.

3) Identify your papers
Civil service exams are usually identified by number only. You will be assigned a number; you must not put your name on your test papers. Be sure to copy your number correctly. Since more than one exam may be given, copy your exact examination title.

4) Plan your time
Unless you are told that a test is a "speed" or "rate of work" test, speed itself is usually not important. Time enough to answer all the questions will be provided, but this does not mean that you have all day. An overall time limit has been set. Divide the total time (in minutes) by the number of questions to determine the approximate time you have for each question.

5) Do not linger over difficult questions

If you come across a difficult question, mark it with a paper clip (useful to have along) and come back to it when you have been through the booklet. One caution if you do this – be sure to skip a number on your answer sheet as well. Check often to be sure that you have not lost your place and that you are marking in the row numbered the same as the question you are answering.

6) Read the questions

Be sure you know what the question asks! Many capable people are unsuccessful because they failed to *read* the questions correctly.

7) Answer all questions

Unless you have been instructed that a penalty will be deducted for incorrect answers, it is better to guess than to omit a question.

8) Speed tests

It is often better NOT to guess on speed tests. It has been found that on timed tests people are tempted to spend the last few seconds before time is called in marking answers at random – without even reading them – in the hope of picking up a few extra points. To discourage this practice, the instructions may warn you that your score will be "corrected" for guessing. That is, a penalty will be applied. The incorrect answers will be deducted from the correct ones, or some other penalty formula will be used.

9) Review your answers

If you finish before time is called, go back to the questions you guessed or omitted to give them further thought. Review other answers if you have time.

10) Return your test materials

If you are ready to leave before others have finished or time is called, take ALL your materials to the monitor and leave quietly. Never take any test material with you. The monitor can discover whose papers are not complete, and taking a test booklet may be grounds for disqualification.

VIII. EXAMINATION TECHNIQUES

1) Read the general instructions carefully. These are usually printed on the first page of the exam booklet. As a rule, these instructions refer to the timing of the examination; the fact that you should not start work until the signal and must stop work at a signal, etc. If there are any *special* instructions, such as a choice of questions to be answered, make sure that you note this instruction carefully.

2) When you are ready to start work on the examination, that is as soon as the signal has been given, read the instructions to each question booklet, underline any key words or phrases, such as *least, best, outline, describe* and the like. In this way you will tend to answer as requested rather than discover on reviewing your paper that you *listed without describing*, that you selected the *worst* choice rather than the *best* choice, etc.

3) If the examination is of the objective or multiple-choice type – that is, each question will also give a series of possible answers: A, B, C or D, and you are called upon to select the best answer and write the letter next to that answer on your answer paper – it is advisable to start answering each question in turn. There may be anywhere from 50 to 100 such questions in the three or four hours allotted and you can see how much time would be taken if you read through all the questions before beginning to answer any. Furthermore, if you come across a question or group of questions which you know would be difficult to answer, it would undoubtedly affect your handling of all the other questions.

4) If the examination is of the essay type and contains but a few questions, it is a moot point as to whether you should read all the questions before starting to answer any one. Of course, if you are given a choice – say five out of seven and the like – then it is essential to read all the questions so you can eliminate the two that are most difficult. If, however, you are asked to answer all the questions, there may be danger in trying to answer the easiest one first because you may find that you will spend too much time on it. The best technique is to answer the first question, then proceed to the second, etc.

5) Time your answers. Before the exam begins, write down the time it started, then add the time allowed for the examination and write down the time it must be completed, then divide the time available somewhat as follows:
   • If 3-1/2 hours are allowed, that would be 210 minutes. If you have 80 objective-type questions, that would be an average of 2-1/2 minutes per question. Allow yourself no more than 2 minutes per question, or a total of 160 minutes, which will permit about 50 minutes to review.
   • If for the time allotment of 210 minutes there are 7 essay questions to answer, that would average about 30 minutes a question. Give yourself only 25 minutes per question so that you have about 35 minutes to review.

6) The most important instruction is to *read each question* and make sure you know what is wanted. The second most important instruction is to *time yourself properly* so that you answer every question. The third most important instruction is to *answer every question*. Guess if you have to but include something for each question. Remember that you will receive no credit for a blank and will probably receive some credit if you write something in answer to an essay question. If you guess a letter – say "B" for a multiple-choice question – you may have guessed right. If you leave a blank as an answer to a multiple-choice question, the examiners may respect your feelings but it will not add a point to your score. Some exams may penalize you for wrong answers, so in such cases *only*, you may not want to guess unless you have some basis for your answer.

7) Suggestions
   a. Objective-type questions
      1. Examine the question booklet for proper sequence of pages and questions
      2. Read all instructions carefully
      3. Skip any question which seems too difficult; return to it after all other questions have been answered
      4. Apportion your time properly; do not spend too much time on any single question or group of questions

9

5. Note and underline key words – *all, most, fewest, least, best, worst, same, opposite,* etc.
6. Pay particular attention to negatives
7. Note unusual option, e.g., unduly long, short, complex, different or similar in content to the body of the question
8. Observe the use of "hedging" words – *probably, may, most likely,* etc.
9. Make sure that your answer is put next to the same number as the question
10. Do not second-guess unless you have good reason to believe the second answer is definitely more correct
11. Cross out original answer if you decide another answer is more accurate; do not erase until you are ready to hand your paper in
12. Answer all questions; guess unless instructed otherwise
13. Leave time for review

    b. Essay questions
      1. Read each question carefully
      2. Determine exactly what is wanted. Underline key words or phrases.
      3. Decide on outline or paragraph answer
      4. Include many different points and elements unless asked to develop any one or two points or elements
      5. Show impartiality by giving pros and cons unless directed to select one side only
      6. Make and write down any assumptions you find necessary to answer the questions
      7. Watch your English, grammar, punctuation and choice of words
      8. Time your answers; don't crowd material

8) Answering the essay question

Most essay questions can be answered by framing the specific response around several key words or ideas. Here are a few such key words or ideas:

M's: manpower, materials, methods, money, management
P's: purpose, program, policy, plan, procedure, practice, problems, pitfalls, personnel, public relations
    a. Six basic steps in handling problems:
      1. Preliminary plan and background development
      2. Collect information, data and facts
      3. Analyze and interpret information, data and facts
      4. Analyze and develop solutions as well as make recommendations
      5. Prepare report and sell recommendations
      6. Install recommendations and follow up effectiveness

    b. Pitfalls to avoid
      1. *Taking things for granted –* A statement of the situation does not necessarily imply that each of the elements is necessarily true; for example, a complaint may be invalid and biased so that all that can be taken for granted is that a complaint has been registered

2. *Considering only one side of a situation* – Wherever possible, indicate several alternatives and then point out the reasons you selected the best one
3. *Failing to indicate follow up* – Whenever your answer indicates action on your part, make certain that you will take proper follow-up action to see how successful your recommendations, procedures or actions turn out to be
4. *Taking too long in answering any single question* – Remember to time your answers properly

IX. AFTER THE TEST

Scoring procedures differ in detail among civil service jurisdictions although the general principles are the same. Whether the papers are hand-scored or graded by machine we have described, they are nearly always graded by number. That is, the person who marks the paper knows only the number – never the name – of the applicant. Not until all the papers have been graded will they be matched with names. If other tests, such as training and experience or oral interview ratings have been given, scores will be combined. Different parts of the examination usually have different weights. For example, the written test might count 60 percent of the final grade, and a rating of training and experience 40 percent. In many jurisdictions, veterans will have a certain number of points added to their grades.

After the final grade has been determined, the names are placed in grade order and an eligible list is established. There are various methods for resolving ties between those who get the same final grade – probably the most common is to place first the name of the person whose application was received first. Job offers are made from the eligible list in the order the names appear on it. You will be notified of your grade and your rank as soon as all these computations have been made. This will be done as rapidly as possible.

People who are found to meet the requirements in the announcement are called "eligibles." Their names are put on a list of eligible candidates. An eligible's chances of getting a job depend on how high he stands on this list and how fast agencies are filling jobs from the list.

When a job is to be filled from a list of eligibles, the agency asks for the names of people on the list of eligibles for that job. When the civil service commission receives this request, it sends to the agency the names of the three people highest on this list. Or, if the job to be filled has specialized requirements, the office sends the agency the names of the top three persons who meet these requirements from the general list.

The appointing officer makes a choice from among the three people whose names were sent to him. If the selected person accepts the appointment, the names of the others are put back on the list to be considered for future openings.

That is the rule in hiring from all kinds of eligible lists, whether they are for typist, carpenter, chemist, or something else. For every vacancy, the appointing officer has his choice of any one of the top three eligibles on the list. This explains why the person whose name is on top of the list sometimes does not get an appointment when some of the persons lower on the list do. If the appointing officer chooses the second or third eligible, the No. 1 eligible does not get a job at once, but stays on the list until he is appointed or the list is terminated.

X. HOW TO PASS THE INTERVIEW TEST

The examination for which you applied requires an oral interview test. You have already taken the written test and you are now being called for the interview test – the final part of the formal examination.

You may think that it is not possible to prepare for an interview test and that there are no procedures to follow during an interview. Our purpose is to point out some things you can do in advance that will help you and some good rules to follow and pitfalls to avoid while you are being interviewed.

What is an interview supposed to test?

The written examination is designed to test the technical knowledge and competence of the candidate; the oral is designed to evaluate intangible qualities, not readily measured otherwise, and to establish a list showing the relative fitness of each candidate – as measured against his competitors – for the position sought. Scoring is not on the basis of "right" and "wrong," but on a sliding scale of values ranging from "not passable" to "outstanding." As a matter of fact, it is possible to achieve a relatively low score without a single "incorrect" answer because of evident weakness in the qualities being measured.

Occasionally, an examination may consist entirely of an oral test – either an individual or a group oral. In such cases, information is sought concerning the technical knowledges and abilities of the candidate, since there has been no written examination for this purpose. More commonly, however, an oral test is used to supplement a written examination.

Who conducts interviews?

The composition of oral boards varies among different jurisdictions. In nearly all, a representative of the personnel department serves as chairman. One of the members of the board may be a representative of the department in which the candidate would work. In some cases, "outside experts" are used, and, frequently, a businessman or some other representative of the general public is asked to serve. Labor and management or other special groups may be represented. The aim is to secure the services of experts in the appropriate field.

However the board is composed, it is a good idea (and not at all improper or unethical) to ascertain in advance of the interview who the members are and what groups they represent. When you are introduced to them, you will have some idea of their backgrounds and interests, and at least you will not stutter and stammer over their names.

What should be done before the interview?

While knowledge about the board members is useful and takes some of the surprise element out of the interview, there is other preparation which is more substantive. It *is* possible to prepare for an oral interview – in several ways:

1) Keep a copy of your application and review it carefully before the interview

This may be the only document before the oral board, and the starting point of the interview. Know what education and experience you have listed there, and the sequence and dates of all of it. Sometimes the board will ask you to review the highlights of your experience for them; you should not have to hem and haw doing it.

2) Study the class specification and the examination announcement

Usually, the oral board has one or both of these to guide them. The qualities, characteristics or knowledges required by the position sought are stated in these documents. They offer valuable clues as to the nature of the oral interview. For example, if the job involves supervisory responsibilities, the announcement will usually indicate that knowledge of modern supervisory methods and the qualifications of the candidate as a supervisor will be tested. If so, you can expect such questions, frequently in the form of a hypothetical situation which you are expected to solve. NEVER go into an oral without knowledge of the duties and responsibilities of the job you seek.

3) Think through each qualification required

Try to visualize the kind of questions you would ask if you were a board member. How well could you answer them? Try especially to appraise your own knowledge and background in each area, *measured against the job sought*, and identify any areas in which you are weak. Be critical and realistic – do not flatter yourself.

4) Do some general reading in areas in which you feel you may be weak

For example, if the job involves supervision and your past experience has NOT, some general reading in supervisory methods and practices, particularly in the field of human relations, might be useful. Do NOT study agency procedures or detailed manuals. The oral board will be testing your understanding and capacity, not your memory.

5) Get a good night's sleep and watch your general health and mental attitude

You will want a clear head at the interview. Take care of a cold or any other minor ailment, and of course, no hangovers.

What should be done on the day of the interview?

Now comes the day of the interview itself. Give yourself plenty of time to get there. Plan to arrive somewhat ahead of the scheduled time, particularly if your appointment is in the fore part of the day. If a previous candidate fails to appear, the board might be ready for you a bit early. By early afternoon an oral board is almost invariably behind schedule if there are many candidates, and you may have to wait. Take along a book or magazine to read, or your application to review, but leave any extraneous material in the waiting room when you go in for your interview. In any event, relax and compose yourself.

The matter of dress is important. The board is forming impressions about you – from your experience, your manners, your attitude, and your appearance. Give your personal appearance careful attention. Dress your best, but not your flashiest. Choose conservative, appropriate clothing, and be sure it is immaculate. This is a business interview, and your appearance should indicate that you regard it as such. Besides, being well groomed and properly dressed will help boost your confidence.

Sooner or later, someone will call your name and escort you into the interview room. *This is it.* From here on you are on your own. It is too late for any more preparation. But remember, you asked for this opportunity to prove your fitness, and you are here because your request was granted.

What happens when you go in?

The usual sequence of events will be as follows: The clerk (who is often the board stenographer) will introduce you to the chairman of the oral board, who will introduce you to the other members of the board. Acknowledge the introductions before you sit down. Do not be surprised if you find a microphone facing you or a stenotypist sitting by. Oral interviews are usually recorded in the event of an appeal or other review.

Usually the chairman of the board will open the interview by reviewing the highlights of your education and work experience from your application – primarily for the benefit of the other members of the board, as well as to get the material into the record. Do not interrupt or comment unless there is an error or significant misinterpretation; if that is the case, do not hesitate. But do not quibble about insignificant matters. Also, he will usually ask you some question about your education, experience or your present job – partly to get you to start talking and to establish the interviewing "rapport." He may start the actual questioning, or turn it over to one of the other members. Frequently, each member undertakes the questioning on a particular area, one in which he is perhaps most competent, so you can expect each member to participate in the examination. Because time is limited, you may also expect some rather abrupt switches in the direction the questioning takes, so do not be upset by it. Normally, a board member will not pursue a single line of questioning unless he discovers a particular strength or weakness.

After each member has participated, the chairman will usually ask whether any member has any further questions, then will ask you if you have anything you wish to add. Unless you are expecting this question, it may floor you. Worse, it may start you off on an extended, extemporaneous speech. The board is not usually seeking more information. The question is principally to offer you a last opportunity to present further qualifications or to indicate that you have nothing to add. So, if you feel that a significant qualification or characteristic has been overlooked, it is proper to point it out in a sentence or so. Do not compliment the board on the thoroughness of their examination – they have been sketchy, and you know it. If you wish, merely say, "No thank you, I have nothing further to add." This is a point where you can "talk yourself out" of a good impression or fail to present an important bit of information. Remember, *you close the interview yourself.*

The chairman will then say, "That is all, Mr. _____, thank you." Do not be startled; the interview is over, and quicker than you think. Thank him, gather your belongings and take your leave. Save your sigh of relief for the other side of the door.

How to put your best foot forward

Throughout this entire process, you may feel that the board individually and collectively is trying to pierce your defenses, seek out your hidden weaknesses and embarrass and confuse you. Actually, this is not true. They are obliged to make an appraisal of your qualifications for the job you are seeking, and they want to see you in your best light. Remember, they must interview all candidates and a non-cooperative candidate may become a failure in spite of their best efforts to bring out his qualifications. Here are 15 suggestions that will help you:

1) Be natural – Keep your attitude confident, not cocky

If you are not confident that you can do the job, do not expect the board to be. Do not apologize for your weaknesses, try to bring out your strong points. The board is interested in a positive, not negative, presentation. Cockiness will antagonize any board member and make him wonder if you are covering up a weakness by a false show of strength.

2) Get comfortable, but don't lounge or sprawl

Sit erectly but not stiffly. A careless posture may lead the board to conclude that you are careless in other things, or at least that you are not impressed by the importance of the occasion. Either conclusion is natural, even if incorrect. Do not fuss with your clothing, a pencil or an ashtray. Your hands may occasionally be useful to emphasize a point; do not let them become a point of distraction.

3) Do not wisecrack or make small talk

This is a serious situation, and your attitude should show that you consider it as such. Further, the time of the board is limited – they do not want to waste it, and neither should you.

4) Do not exaggerate your experience or abilities

In the first place, from information in the application or other interviews and sources, the board may know more about you than you think. Secondly, you probably will not get away with it. An experienced board is rather adept at spotting such a situation, so do not take the chance.

5) If you know a board member, do not make a point of it, yet do not hide it

Certainly you are not fooling him, and probably not the other members of the board. Do not try to take advantage of your acquaintanceship – it will probably do you little good.

6) Do not dominate the interview

Let the board do that. They will give you the clues – do not assume that you have to do all the talking. Realize that the board has a number of questions to ask you, and do not try to take up all the interview time by showing off your extensive knowledge of the answer to the first one.

7) Be attentive

You only have 20 minutes or so, and you should keep your attention at its sharpest throughout. When a member is addressing a problem or question to you, give him your undivided attention. Address your reply principally to him, but do not exclude the other board members.

8) Do not interrupt

A board member may be stating a problem for you to analyze. He will ask you a question when the time comes. Let him state the problem, and wait for the question.

9) Make sure you understand the question

Do not try to answer until you are sure what the question is. If it is not clear, restate it in your own words or ask the board member to clarify it for you. However, do not haggle about minor elements.

10) Reply promptly but not hastily

A common entry on oral board rating sheets is "candidate responded readily," or "candidate hesitated in replies." Respond as promptly and quickly as you can, but do not jump to a hasty, ill-considered answer.

11) Do not be peremptory in your answers

A brief answer is proper – but do not fire your answer back. That is a losing game from your point of view. The board member can probably ask questions much faster than you can answer them.

12) Do not try to create the answer you think the board member wants

He is interested in what kind of mind you have and how it works – not in playing games. Furthermore, he can usually spot this practice and will actually grade you down on it.

13) Do not switch sides in your reply merely to agree with a board member

Frequently, a member will take a contrary position merely to draw you out and to see if you are willing and able to defend your point of view. Do not start a debate, yet do not surrender a good position. If a position is worth taking, it is worth defending.

14) Do not be afraid to admit an error in judgment if you are shown to be wrong

The board knows that you are forced to reply without any opportunity for careful consideration. Your answer may be demonstrably wrong. If so, admit it and get on with the interview.

15) Do not dwell at length on your present job

The opening question may relate to your present assignment. Answer the question but do not go into an extended discussion. You are being examined for a *new* job, not your present one. As a matter of fact, try to phrase ALL your answers in terms of the job for which you are being examined.

Basis of Rating

Probably you will forget most of these "do's" and "don'ts" when you walk into the oral interview room. Even remembering them all will not ensure you a passing grade. Perhaps you did not have the qualifications in the first place. But remembering them will help you to put your best foot forward, without treading on the toes of the board members.

Rumor and popular opinion to the contrary notwithstanding, an oral board wants you to make the best appearance possible. They know you are under pressure – but they also want to see how you respond to it as a guide to what your reaction would be under the pressures of the job you seek. They will be influenced by the degree of poise you display, the personal traits you show and the manner in which you respond.

ABOUT THIS BOOK

This book contains tests divided into Examination Sections. Go through each test, answering every question in the margin. We have also attached a sample answer sheet at the back of the book that can be removed and used. At the end of each test look at the answer key and check your answers. On the ones you got wrong, look at the right answer choice and learn. Do not fill in the answers first. Do not memorize the questions and answers, but understand the answer and principles involved. On your test, the questions will likely be different from the samples. Questions are changed and new ones added. If you understand these past questions you should have success with any changes that arise. Tests may consist of several types of questions. We have additional books on each subject should more study be advisable or necessary for you. Finally, the more you study, the better prepared you will be. This book is intended to be the last thing you study before you walk into the examination room. Prior study of relevant texts is also recommended. NLC publishes some of these in our Fundamental Series. Knowledge and good sense are important factors in passing your exam. Good luck also helps. So now study this Passbook, absorb the material contained within and take that knowledge into the examination. Then do your best to pass that exam.

———

EXAMINATION SECTION

EXAMINATION SECTION
TEST 1

DIRECTIONS: Each question or incomplete statement is followed by several suggested answers or completions. Select the one that BEST answers the question or completes the statement. *PRINT THE LETTER OF THE CORRECT ANSWER IN THE SPACE AT THE RIGHT.*

1. On the monthly report of the amount of work completed, the units used to measure the amount of work completed on guardrails and beam barriers installed on arterial highways is

    A. square feet   B. square yards
    C. linear feet   D. linear yards

1.____

2. On the daily work report for the sidewalk concrete gang is a formula, $M = [G - (D + U)]$, where G = total man-hours worked, D = total man-hours delays, U = total man-hours unmeasured work, and M = total man-hours measured work.
If G = 98, D = 42, U = 21, then M is equal to

    A. 35   B. 56   C. 77   D. 119

2.____

3. When a plumber *opens a street*, he is responsible for restoring the pavement. After completion of the permanent restoration, the plumber is responsible for maintaining the restored area for a total period of

    A. six months   B. one year
    C. one year and 6 months   D. two years

3.____

4. A permit for a street opening may be issued for a single permit activity for one block length up to a MAXIMUM length of _____ feet.

    A. 50   B. 100   C. 200   D. 300

4.____

5. A street obstruction bond taken out by a contractor working in the street is to insure the city if

    A. a pedestrian is injured by material stored on the sidewalk
    B. an automobile is damaged by material stored in the street
    C. curbs, sidewalks, and pavements are damaged
    D. obstructions, illegally placed in the street, must be removed

5.____

6. On the daily work report for the sidewalk concrete gang is an item *curb*.
The different types of curb listed on the report are: bluestone or granite, concrete-steel face, concrete-regular face, and

    A. drop   B. paving block
    C. concrete block   D. prefabricated

6.____

7. On the monthly report of work output under time (manhours) is a column headed MSO, which refers to manhours

    A. of mechanical services operator other than MVO
    B. of operation time lost while waiting
    C. of operation time lost due to the weather
    D. spent operating mechanical equipment by the MVO

7.____

8. In the city, concrete sidewalks are required to have a minimum thickness of concrete of _____ inches.

    A. 3   B. 4   C. 5   D. 6

8.__

9. Asphalt was laid for a length of 210 feet on the entire width of a street whose curb-to-curb distance is 30 feet. The number of square yards covered with asphalt is MOST NEARLY

    A. 210   B. 700   C. 2100   D. 6300

9.__

10. A layer of cinders is used as a base for a concrete sidewalk.
The MAIN purpose of the cinders is to

    A. act as an air entraining agent for the concrete in the sidewalk
    B. replace poor soil under the sidewalk
    C. provide drainage under the sidewalk
    D. cushion the sidewalk when heavy loads are placed on the sidewalk

10.__

11. The unit used on the daily gang report to report the amount of measurement of debris removed is

    A. square foot   B. square yard
    C. cubic foot   D. cubic yard

11.__

12. 627 cubic feet contains MOST NEARLY _____ cubic yards.

    A. 21   B. 22   C. 23   D. 24

12.__

13. Of the following, the one that is INCORRECT curb construction is a curb made

    A. with a height of 5 inches
    B. with a steel angle for the face
    C. without a steel face
    D. monolithically with the sidewalk

13.__

14. Where feasible, concrete sidewalk panels should be made in squares of _____ feet by _____ feet.

    A. 3; 3   B. 5; 5   C. 6; 6   D. 7; 7

14.__

15. The steel facing for concrete curbs are splayed

    A. at an expansion joint
    B. where it butts against an adjacent steel plate
    C. at a drop curb
    D. at a radius bend

15.__

16. Expansion joints in steel curb facing shall be 1/4 inch wide and shall be filled with

    A. sand   B. premolded filler
    C. poured asphalt   D. dry pack

16.__

17. One inch is MOST NEARLY equal to _____ feet.

    A. 0.8   B. 0.08   C. 0.008   D. 0.0008

17.__

18. Of the following, the *final* finish on a sidewalk is MOST frequently made with a   18.____

    A. wood float   B. screed
    C. steel trowel   D. darby

19. An air entraining compound would be added to concrete MAINLY to   19.____

    A. make the concrete lighter
    B. make the concrete cure faster
    C. improve the resistance of the concrete to frost action
    D. increase the tensile strength of the concrete

20. *ASTM,* as used in specifications for concrete, is an abbreviation for the   20.____

    A. American Society for Testing Materials
    B. American Standard Training Manual
    C. American Standard Testing Materials
    D. Association of Scientists for Testing Materials

21. A 15-foot-wide sidewalk has a pitch of 1/4 inch per foot. The difference in elevation from   21.____
the curb to 15 feet from the curb in the direction of the pitch is _____ inches.

    A. 3   B. 3 3/4   C. 4   D. 4 1/2

22. A liquid asphalt is designated *RC70.*   22.____
The letters RC stand for

    A. Rough Course   B. Rubber Cement
    C. Rapid Curing   D. Reinforced Concrete

23. Unless otherwise specified, steel faced concrete curb shall consist of the steel curb fac-   23.____
ing in _____-foot lengths.

    A. 5   B. 10   C. 15   D. 20

24. The difference between sheet asphalt and asphaltic concrete is that sheet asphalt   24.____

    A. contains no sand while asphaltic concrete contains sand
    B. contains no coarse aggregate while asphaltic concrete contains coarse aggregate
    C. contains no mineral filler while asphaltic concrete contains mineral filler
    D. has no flux while asphaltic concrete has flux

25. An approved roller shall weigh not less than 225 pounds per inch width of main roll.   25.____
If the main roll width is 60 inches, the MINIMUM roller weight shall be equal to or
greater than _____ lbs.

    A. 12,000   B. 12,500   C. 13,000   D. 13,500

KEY (CORRECT ANSWERS)

1.	C	11.	D
2.	A	12.	C
3.	D	13.	D
4.	D	14.	B
5.	C	15.	C
6.	A	16.	B
7.	A	17.	B
8.	B	18.	A
9.	B	19.	C
10.	C	20.	A

21.	B
22.	C
23.	D
24.	B
25.	D

———

TEST 2

DIRECTIONS: Each question or incomplete statement is followed by several suggested answers or completions. Select the one that BEST answers the question or completes the statement. *PRINT THE LETTER OF THE CORRECT ANSWER IN THE SPACE AT THE RIGHT.*

1. A specification states that the rate of application of asphalt cement shall be 1 1/2 gallons per square yard with a tolerance of 1/10 of a gallon.
   Of the following, the rate of application that would be acceptable is _____ gallons per square yard.

   A. 1.2   B. 1.3   C. 1.6   D. 1.7

   1.____

2. Of the following, the BEST reason for compacting backfill is to

   A. prevent settlement   B. crush oversized rocks
   C. facilitate drainage   D. make the soil uniform

   2.____

3. Asphalt block is hexagonal tile block.
   The number of vertical sides of each block in place is

   A. 4   B. 6   C. 8   D. 10

   3.____

4. Concrete driveways shall have a MINIMUM thickness of concrete of _____ inches.

   A. 5   B. 6   C. 7   D. 8

   4.____

5. When the tops of manholes must be raised because of repaving, the MOST practical of the following methods to use is to

   A. break out the manhole frame and replace it with a deeper frame
   B. remove the manhole frame, build up the top of the manhole with bricks, and reset the frame
   C. use a thicker manhole cover
   D. place a metal collar on top of the existing frame

   5.____

6. In a 1:2:4 concrete mix, the 2 indicates the quantity of

   A. water   B. sand   C. cement   D. aggregate

   6.____

7. A tree pit shall be located in the area immediately in back of the curb.
   The MAXIMUM size of the tree pit shall be

   A. 3' x 3'   B. 4' x 4'   C. 5' x 5'   D. 6' x 6'

   7.____

8. A temporary asphaltic pavement is placed over an excavation in the street by a private contractor.
   The MINIMUM required thickness of the finish course of the temporary asphaltic pavement is _____ inch(es).

   A. 1   B. 2   C. 3   D. 4

   8.____

9. When a vault is abandoned, it must be filled in with clean incombustible materials, well-tamped.
   Where such structures adjoin the curb of a street, the roof must be removed and the enclosing walls cut down below the curb to a depth of _____ feet.

   A. 2   B. 4   C. 6   D. 8

   9.____

10. Granite curbs are required to be set on a cradle. The MAIN purpose of the cradle is to   10.___

    A. prevent cracking of the curb
    B. prevent settling of the curb
    C. help keep the curb in line while it is being set
    D. separate the curb from the adjacent sidewalk

11. Paving was installed on a street from Station 3+15 to Station 4+90.   11.___
The length of street that was paved is _____ feet.

    A. 75   B. 115   C. 175   D. 215

12. A district foreman uses an engineer's tape and measures a distance of 26.50 feet.   12.___
This distance is equal to _____ feet _____ inch(es).

    A. 26; 5   B. 26; 6   C. 26; 1/2   D. 26; 0.6

13. Written on a can containing material delivered from a manufacturer is the notation   13.___
Approved by the B.S. & A.
The B.S. & A. is an abbreviation for the

    A. Bureau of Shipping and Allocation
    B. Board of Standards and Appeals
    C. Board of Supervision and Approval
    D. Bureau of Supervision and Assistance

14. An asphalt macadam pavement consists of a base course and a wearing course.   14.___
The purpose of the base course is to

    A. provide drainage
    B. provide a level surface for the wearing course
    C. spread the load from the surface when it reaches the soil
    D. replace defective soil

15. Of the following, the MOST important recent advancement in power-driven equipment   15.___
and tools is

    A. reduction in weight of the equipment
    B. improved surface finish
    C. higher operating speed
    D. lower noise levels

16. A wooden horse, used to warn traffic away, should be placed in front of which of the fol-   16.___
lowing defects in the street?
A

    A. broken curb
    B. piece of roadway pavement that is very thin and the pavement whose base is start-
ing to show through
    C. very badly broken manhole cover in the center of the street
    D. catch basin filled to the surface with debris

17. When a street is to be paved, the roller should   17.____

    A.   start at the curb, go the length of the street and then move toward the center
    B.   move from curb to curb transversely across the street
    C.   start at the center, go the length of the street, and then move toward the curb
    D.   roll at all the manhole covers first and then start rolling the length of the street

18. The use of long chutes to place concrete for a road base is usually prohibited.   18.____
The BEST of the following reasons for prohibiting long chutes in this case is that

    A.   the concrete will set by the time it is in place
    B.   the water will evaporate from the mix
    C.   segregation of the aggregate will occur
    D.   the stone will be broken down into smaller particles

19. When sheet asphalt is spread by hand, the speed of the rolling should NOT exceed   19.____
_____ square yards per hour.

    A.   100   B.   300   C.   500   D.   700

20. Of the following, the BEST way to insure long trouble-free operation of mechanical equip-   20.____
ment is by periodic inspection and

    A.   use   B.   servicing
    C.   painting   D.   rotation of operators

21. Of the following maintenance work, the one type that is LEAST likely to be done by your   21.____
agency on mechanical equipment is

    A.   tune-up   B.   repairing
    C.   overhauling   D.   rebuilding

22. Of the following, the MOST important equipment needed to lay sheet asphalt pavement   22.____
is truck, roller, fire wagon, and

    A.   grader   B.   distributor
    C.   planer   D.   spreader

23. Of the following, the BEST reason why deep potholes should be repaired *immediately* is   23.____
that

    A.   they look bad
    B.   they are a safety hazard
    C.   they present a drainage problem
    D.   people complaining about unfilled potholes cause unfavorable publicity

24. Of the following, the MOST serious safety hazard on highway and street maintenance   24.____
work is

    A.   injury from flying debris during pavement breaking
    B.   motor traffic
    C.   working close to trucks, bulldozers, and rollers
    D.   cave-ins

25. Of the following, the BEST way a laborer can avoid accidents is to   25.____

    A. work slowly   B. be alert
    C. wear safety shoes   D. wear glasses

26. Of the following, the BEST first aid treatment for a second degree burn is to cover the   26.____
burn with a _____ sterile dressing.

    A. thin, wet   B. thin, dry
    C. thick, wet   D. thick, dry

27. One of the laborers on the job feels unusually tired, has a headache and nausea, is per-   27.____
spiring heavily, and the skin is pale and clammy.
He is probably suffering from

    A. epilepsy   B. food poisoning
    C. heat exhaustion   D. sunstroke

28. If a laborer feels faint, the BEST advice to give him is to advise him to   28.____

    A. lie flat with his head low
    B. walk around till he revives
    C. run around till he revives
    D. drink a glass of cold water

29. Of the following types of fire extinguisher, the one to use on an electrical fire is   29.____

    A. soda acid   B. carbon dioxide
    C. water pump tank   D. pyrene

30. The GREATEST number of injuries from equipment used in construction work result from   30.____

    A. carelessness of the operator
    B. poor maintenance of the equipment
    C. overloading of the equipment
    D. poor inspection of the equipment

KEY (CORRECT ANSWERS)

1.	C	16.	C
2.	A	17.	A
3.	B	18.	C
4.	C	19.	B
5.	D	20.	B
6.	B	21.	D
7.	C	22.	D
8.	C	23.	B
9.	A	24.	B
10.	B	25.	B
11.	C	26.	D
12.	B	27.	C
13.	B	28.	A
14.	C	29.	B
15.	D	30.	A

EXAMINATION SECTION
TEST 1

DIRECTIONS: Each question or incomplete statement is followed by several suggested answers or completions. Select the one that BEST answers the question or completes the statement. *PRINT THE LETTER OF THE CORRECT ANSWER IN THE SPACE AT THE RIGHT.*

1. The top course of an asphalt pavement is called the _____ course.   1.____

    A. base   B. binder
    C. water-proofing   D. wearing

2. The MAIN reason for heating materials used in asphalt paving is that   2.____

    A. the impurities can be burned out
    B. the poor quality asphalt can be separated out
    C. their wearing qualities can be increased
    D. they can be mixed and handled properly

3. In laying an asphalt wearing surface, the finished surface is USUALLY bonded to the con-   3.____
   crete base by a(n)

    A. asphaltic cement and stone binder
    B. coat of tar
    C. layer of plain asphalt
    D. Portland cement grout

4. The surface of an asphalt which is being heated is foaming.   4.____
   The temperature of the asphalt is 200 ° F.
   The foaming indicates that

    A. there is water present in the asphalt
    B. the asphalt is overheated
    C. asphalt is not hot enough
    D. vessel in which asphalt is being heated is too small

5. Traffic should NOT be allowed on a completed asphaltic concrete pavement   5.____

    A. until the mixture has cooled
    B. for 2 days
    C. for 7 days
    D. for 30 days

6. A penetration test has been performed with a standard needle on an asphaltic material.   6.____
   In reporting the test, it is NOT necessary to specify

    A. loading of needle
    B. time required for penetration
    C. thickness of sample
    D. temperature of sample

7. Water-cement ratio is USUALLY expressed in   7.____

    A. cubic feet per cubic foot   B. gallons per sack
    C. pounds per cubic foot   D. gallons per pound

8. Surface moisture is all water   8.___

    A. carried by the aggregate
    B. absorbed by the aggregate particles
    C. carried by the aggregate other than that absorbed by the aggregate particles
    D. except that carried by the aggregate

9. A quick-setting emulsified asphalt would MOST likely be used for   9.___

    A. coarse aggregate mixes   B. retread mixes
    C. heavy premix   D. joint filler

10. Asphaltic cement for asphaltic concrete should be heated, before mixing with aggregate,   10.___
    to a temperature of

    A. 150 ° F   B. 225 ° F   C. 300 ° F   D. 375 ° F

11. The temperature of sand to be used in ordinary asphaltic concrete, when delivered to the   11.___
    weighing box, should NOT exceed

    A. 1250 ° F   B. 225 ° F   C. 325 ° F   D. 525 ° F

12. The temperature of an ordinary sheet asphalt mix, when delivered on the street, should   12.___
    NOT be less than

    A. 325 ° F   B. 275 ° F   C. 225 ° F   D. 175 ° F

13. When a sheet asphalt pavement is being constructed, contact surfaces should be   13.___
    painted

    A. *before* the binder course is laid
    B. *before* the surface course is laid
    C. *before* the surface course is rolled
    D. *after* the surface course is rolled

14. The use of smoothing irons on the surface of sheet asphalt pavements is usually NOT   14.___
    permitted

    A. at joints
    B. to smooth irregularities in the surface
    C. at contact surfaces
    D. to iron in hot asphaltic cement on a strip adjacent to the curb

15. Rolling of the surface mixture of a sheet asphalt pavement should be continued until all   15.___
    but one of the following conditions are met.
    The condition which need NOT be met is the one wherein

    A. the mixture has cooled
    B. no marks show under the roller
    C. the pavement is free from waves
    D. the surface has been tested with an approved straight edge or surface testing
       machine

16. In determining the area of pavement to be paid for, the areas of the spaces occupied by   16._____
column bases, manhole heads, gate boxes, and similar structures are

    A. not deducted from the gross area
    B. deducted from the gross area
    C. deducted only if the area occupied by a structure exceeds one square foot
    D. deducted only if the area occupied by a structure is less than one square foot

17. Concrete base for pavement is specified to be ten inches thick.   17._____
Around manhole heads and similar structures, this base should have a depth, in
inches, of

    A. 12   B. 10   C. 8   D. 6

18. Cores taken from a concrete base for pavement 40 ft. wide by 250 ft. long have the fol-   18._____

lowing thicknesses: 8 1/8", 8 3/8", 7 3/4", and 8 1/4".

The volume of concrete to be paid for is, in cubic yards, MOST NEARLY

    A. 251   B. 255   C. 259   D. 263

19. The slump of concrete to be used for a pavement base should be, in inches, about   19._____

    A. 7   B. 8 1/4   C. 4   D. 2 1/2

20. Adhesion of asphaltic material to the rolls of a roller is prevented by spraying the rolls   20._____
with

    A. water   B. heavy oil   C. gasoline   D. naphtha

21. Of the following, the one which would NOT normally be used for a base or binder course   21._____
is

    A. water-bound macadam   B. asphalt macadam
    C. asphaltic concrete   D. sheet asphalt

22. Some specifications require that the roller weigh not less than 225 lbs. per inch width of   22._____
main roll while others require the roller weigh not less than ten tons.
It is CORRECT to say that the first type of specification

    A. permits the use of rollers too light for the job
    B. will probably obtain more uniform compaction by a group of contractors
    C. may result in the use of rollers which are too wide
    D. may result in the use of rollers which are too heavy

23. The MOST stable macadam base course will probably result if the material used consists   23._____
of

    A. angular pieces of freshly broken rock
    B. angular pieces of rock which has weathered after breaking
    C. bank-run gravel
    D. rounded pieces of freshly broken gravel

24. A pavement 40 feet wide between curbs which are at the same elevation has a crown of 5 inches. One end of a straight board 10 ft. long is placed on the pavement at the center line of the pavement. The board is leveled and runs perpendicular to the curb.
The vertical space between the board and the pavement at the other end is, in inches, about

    A. 5   B. 3 ¾   C. 2 ½   D. 1 ¼

24.__

25. A sheet asphalt pavement has been cut for a water connection. The width of cut in the asphalt is the same as that in the concrete base.
The FIRST thing to do after the concrete base has been repaired and has hardened is to

    A. paint the edges of the asphalt
    B. cut the asphalt back several inches from the edges of the concrete patch
    C. soften the edges of the asphalt with a surface heater
    D. heat the edges of the asphalt with a smoothing iron

25.__

———————

KEY (CORRECT ANSWERS)

1.	D		11.	C
2.	D		12.	B
3.	A		13.	B
4.	A		14.	B
5.	A		15.	D
6.	C		16.	C
7.	B		17.	A
8.	C		18.	A
9.	D		19.	D
10.	C		20.	A

21.	D
22.	B
23.	A
24.	D
25.	B

———————

EXAMINATION SECTION
TEST 1

DIRECTIONS: Each question or incomplete statement is followed by several suggested answers or completions. Select the one that BEST answers the question or completes the statement. *PRINT THE LETTER OF THE CORRECT ANSWER IN THE SPACE AT THE RIGHT.*

1. Asphalt is derived mainly

   A. as a byproduct from the production of coke
   B. from asphalt deposits seeping to the surface of the earth
   C. from the refining of crude oil
   D. from bituminous coal

1.____

2. Cutback liquid asphalts are prepared by blending asphalt with a volatile solvent. The one of the following that is NOT used as an asphalt solvent is

   A. naphtha   B. gasoline   C. kerosene   D. toluene

2.____

3. The primary purpose of the solvent in cutback asphalt is to allow the

   A. use of a larger size aggregate in the mix
   B. application of the asphalt at a relatively low temperature
   C. application of asphalt in wet weather
   D. application of asphalt in hot weather

3.____

4. The thickness of the sheet asphalt on a sheet asphalt pavement is usually _____ inch(es).

   A. 1/2 inch to 3/4   B. 1 inch to 1 1/2
   C. 1 5/8 inches to 2   D. 2 1/4 inches to 3

4.____

5. The grade of an asphalt cement is designated as AR4000.
The AR is an abbreviation for

   A. asphalt rating   B. acid resistance
   C. aged residue   D. aging resistance

5.____

6. An asphaltic emulsion is a suspension of asphalt in

   A. kerosene   B. gasoline   C. toluene   D. water

6.____

7. A very light application of asphalt on an existing paved surface will promote bond between this surface and the subsequent course is known as a(n) _____ coat.

   A. prime   B. adhesion
   C. tack   D. penetrating

7.____

8. Of the following, payment is usually made for asphalt pavements at the contract price per

   A. square inch   B. square foot
   C. square yard   D. 100 square feet

8.____

9. The grade of an asphalt cement is designated AR4000.
The 4000 is a measure of   9.___

   A. strength   B. viscosity   C. ductility   D. density

10. Of the following, the geometric shape of a horizontal curve on a highway is 10.___

   A. parabolic   B. hyperbolic
   C. circular   D. elliptical

11. A borrow pit in highway construction is used 11.___

   A. for storing stormwater in a heavy rain
   B. for coarse aggregate in Portland cement concrete
   C. for coarse aggregate in asphalt concrete
   D. to obtain fill for embankments

12. Overhaul in highway construction is usually measured and paid for by the 12.___

   A. yard - cubic foot   B. yard - cubic yard
   C. station - cubic foot   D. station - cubic yard

13. A Benkelman beam is used in highway work 13.___

   A. as an indicator of the ability of a pavement to withstand loading
   B. to measure the roughness of an asphalt concrete pavement
   C. to measure the uniformity of an asphalt concrete pavement
   D. to measure the ability of an asphalt concrete pavement to remain serviceable if the subgrade is undermined

14. When surfacing over an existing pavement, of the following, the MOST practical way to insure that the required thickness of new pavement is met is 14.___

   A. expansion of clay when exposed to water
   B. expansion of soil when excavated
   C. waviness in a soil embankment when being compacted with a roller
   D. expansion of loamy soil when exposed to water

15. When surfacing over an existing pavement, of the following, the MOST practical way to insure that the required thickness of new pavement is met is 15.___

   A. have wood blocks of the thickness of the new pavement temporarily placed on the existing pavement to insure that the thickness requirements will be met at the time of paving
   B. make a survey of the existing pavement elevations and a survey of the final pavement elevations and check that the thickness requirements are met
   C. check that the amount of asphalt delivered is adequate to meet the depth requirements of the area to be paved
   D. take core borings to determine if the thickness meets specifications

16. The maximum roller speed for steel tired rollers paving asphalt concrete is a maximum of _____ mile(s) per hour. 16.___

   A. 7   B. 5   C. 3   D. 1

17. The weathered or dry surface appearing on a relatively new pavement can generally be attributed to

    A.   inadequate rolling
    B.   oversized coarse aggregate in the mix
    C.   excessive amount of fine aggregate
    D.   insufficient asphalt in the mix

17._____

18. Construction contracts for highways have items paid either by unit price or lump sum. The one of the following that is usually a lump sum item on a highway contract is

    A.   excavation   B.   paving
    C.   fencing   D.   demolition

18._____

19. Highway roadway subgrades are usually required to have a relative density of _____ percent.

    A.   80 to 84   B.   85 to 89   C.   90 to 95   D.   100

19._____

20. A *profile* of a highway is

    A.   the section taken along the centerline of the highway
    B.   an aesthetic landscape sketch of the highway
    C.   used to determine the line of the highway
    D.   used to locate overpasses

20._____

21. A culvert as used under a highway is usually installed

    A.   as a relief sewer
    B.   as a bypass for a stream
    C.   in a stream bed
    D.   to carry sanitary and storm flow

21._____

22. A mass diagram as related to highway construction work is used to

    A.   minimize traffic congestion
    B.   compute payment for hauling excavation and fill
    C.   find the largest feasible radius of curvature for a horizontal curve
    D.   help determine the depth of an asphalt concrete pavement

22._____

23. The geometric shape of a vertical curve on a highway is a(n)

    A.   parabola   B.   hyperbola   C.   circle   D.   ellipse

23._____

24. When cast iron bell and spigot pipe is used in sewer construction, the joint is usually sealed with

    A.   lead   B.   tin
    C.   cement mortar   D.   oakum

24._____

25. A planimeter is used to measure

    A.   location   B.   area   C.   elevation   D.   angles

25._____

KEY (CORRECT ANSWERS)

1.	C	11.	D
2.	D	12.	D
3.	B	13.	A
4.	B	14.	B
5.	C	15.	A
6.	D	16.	C
7.	C	17.	D
8.	B	18.	D
9.	B	19.	C
10.	C	20.	A

21.	C
22.	B
23.	A
24.	A
25.	B

TEST 2

DIRECTIONS: Each question or incomplete statement is followed by several suggested answers or completions. Select the one that BEST answers the question or completes the statement. *PRINT THE LETTER OF THE CORRECT ANSWER IN THE SPACE AT THE RIGHT.*

1. A witness stake is usually used in surveying primarily as   1.____

    A. proof that a given location has been surveyed
    B. an aid in locating a surveying stake
    C. a marker to prevent a stake being disturbed
    D. an offset stake

2. Before the contractor begins work on a sewer or highway project, a detailed survey is   2.____
   made of all existing structures that may be affected by the construction in order to

    A. protect against false claims for damage
    B. insure that the contractor causes no damage to property
    C. insure that existing elevations conform to elevations on the contract drawings
    D. uncover potential weaknesses in structures

3. The optimum moisture content of a given soil will result in the   3.____

    A. plastic limit of the soil is reached
    B. liquid limit of the soil is reached
    C. porosity of the soil is at its maximum
    D. soil is compacted to its maximum dry density

4. The letters SC for soil means   4.____

    A. silty clay   B. clayey sand
    C. sandy clay   D. clayey silt

5. A cradle is used under a large precast circular concrete pipe sewer. The purpose of the   5.____
   cradle is mainly to

    A. minimize the settlement of the earth on the sides of the sewer
    B. minimize the settlement under the pipe
    C. strengthen the pipe against collapse
    D. resist side pressure against the pipe

6. The joints on laid precast concrete pipe were poorly made.   6.____
   The consequence of this poor workmanship is most likely

    A. the pipe will settle
    B. the pipe may collapse
    C. the water table may be adversely affected
    D. there will be excessive infiltration

7. An existing sewer is to connect into a new deep manhole for a new sewer. According to   7.____
   old plans for the existing sewer, the elevation of the existing sewer is 1/2 inch lower than
   shown on the plan.
   Of the following, the BEST action that the inspector can take is

A.   call his superior for instructions
B.   do nothing
C.   have the contractor relay the existing pipe to the theoretical elevation shown on the old plan
D.   have an adjustable connection placed between the old pipe and the new manhole

8.   The contractor proposes using a cement-lime mix for cement mortar to be used in building a manhole.
This is   8.____

A.   *good* practice as this is a more workable mortar
B.   *good* practice as the mortar is slow setting
C.   *poor* practice because the mortar weakens in a wet environment
D.   *poor* practice as a cement-lime mortar is more porous than a cement mortar

9.   Most serious claims for extra payment on large sewer contracts result from   9.____

A.   soil conditions that are markedly different from those that were presented by the owner
B.   the inspectors being unreasonable in their demands
C.   delay in making the areas available for work
D.   the fact that the method of construction required by the owner proved to be unworkable

10.   Unconsolidated fill is at pipe laying depth. Of the following, the BEST action that an inspector can take is to   10.____

A.   have the unconsolidated fill removed and replaced with concrete
B.   have the unconsolidated fill removed and replaced with sound fill
C.   report this matter to your supervisor for his consideration
D.   ask the contractor to consolidate the fill

11.   Buried debris not shown on the borings is uncovered near the surface of an excavation for a deep sewer. Of the following, the BEST action for an inspector to take is to   11.____

A.   record the depth and extent of the debris in the event of a claim
B.   do nothing as this has no effect on the final product
C.   notify the contractor that there is no valid claim for the extra work required
D.   be certain that the debris is not used in the backfill

12.   A come-along or deadman is sometimes used in the laying of large precast concrete pipe to insure   12.____

A.   the pipe is at proper grade
B.   the pipe is on proper line
C.   that the pipe will not subsequently settle
D.   that the pipe is properly seated

13.   In laying sewers,   13.____

A.   accuracy in the line of the sewer is more important than accuracy in the grade of the sewer
B.   accuracy in the grade of the sewer is more important than accuracy in the line of the sewer

C. accuracy in the line and grade of the sewer are equally important
D. since the sewer is underground, accuracy is not required either for line or grade

14. A sewer contract is given out with a price per foot of sewer for different diameter sewers. After the contract is let, the low bidder is required to give a breakdown of his price per foot of sewer to include excavation, sewer in place, backfill, and restoration. The purpose of this breakdown is to

    14.____

A. facilitate partial payments
B. insure the bid is not unbalanced
C. enable the agency to gather up-to-date cost data for future projects
D. make it easier to price extra work

15. The house sewer runs from the house to the main line sewer. The size of this sewer is most frequently _____ inches.

    15.____

A. 4   B. 5   C. 6   D. 8

16. A line on centerline at the inside bottom of a pipe or conduit is known as the

    16.____

A. convert   B. invert   C. subvert   D. exvert

17. One of the most important elements of excavating for sewer construction is to maintain the specified width of the trench at the top of the pipe. If the width at the top of the pipe is too great,

    17.____

A. this may cause excessive settlement of the pipe
B. this may cause excessive settlement of the backfill damaging the final pavement
C. this may place excessive load on the pipe
D. it may undermine utilities adjacent to the pipe

18. Wellpoints are used in sewer construction mainly to

    18.____

A. keep water out of the trench due to a heavy rainstorm
B. keep water out of the excavation and subsoil to avoid excessive pressure on the sheeting
C. prevent a boil from forming in the trench
D. lower the water table to facilitate construction of the sewer

19. When a trench excavation uses soldier beams and horizontal sheeting for support, the minimum number of braces for each soldier beam is

    19.____

A. 1   B. 2   C. 3   D. 4

20. Bell and spigot pipe should be laid _____ with the bell end pointed _____.

    20.____

A. downstream; upstream   B. downstream; downstream
C. upstream; upstream   D. upstream; downstream

21. The specifications state that house sewers should be laid at a grade of not less than 2%. In 40 feet of house sewer, the change in grade for 40 feet should be most nearly _____ inches.

    21.____

A. 8   B. 8 1/2   C. 9   D. 9 1/2

22. Two percent grade on a house sewer is equal to most nearly _____ inch per foot.   22.____

    A. 1/8   B. 3/16   C. 1/4   D. 5/16

23. When working underground in spaces that are closed and confined, such as manholes,   23.____
the gas that is dangerous and most likely of the following to be present is

    A. carbon monoxide   B. carbon dioxide
    C. ammonia   D. methane

24. Of the following, air entrained cement would most likely be used in   24.____

    A. concrete roadways
    B. precast concrete pipe
    C. precast concrete manholes
    D. the cradle for precast concrete pipe

25. A slump cone is filled to overflowing in _____ layer(s).   25.____

    A. one   B. two separate
    C. three separate   D. four separate

—————

KEY (CORRECT ANSWERS)

1.	B	11.	A
2.	A	12.	D
3.	D	13.	B
4.	B	14.	A
5.	B	15.	C
6.	D	16.	B
7.	B	17.	C
8.	C	18.	D
9.	A	19.	B
10.	C	20.	C

21.	D
22.	C
23.	D
24.	A
25.	C

—————

EXAMINATION SECTION
TEST 1

DIRECTIONS: Each question or incomplete statement is followed by several suggested answers or completions. Select the one that BEST answers the question or completes the statement. *PRINT THE LETTER OF THE CORRECT ANSWER IN THE SPACE AT THE RIGHT.*

1. Reinforcing steel is coated with epoxy primarily to _____ of the steel.   1._____

    A.   prevent corrosion
    B.   improve the electric conductivity
    C.   increase the tensile strength
    D.   increase the compressive strength

2. Specifications for concrete require that concrete shall reach or exceed the design   2._____
   strength at the end of days.

    A.   14   B.   21   C.   28   D.   35

3. A #G reinforcing bar has a cross-section area of square inches.   3._____

    A.   .44   B.   .48   C.   .52   D.   .56

4. Mixing time for concrete which is measured from the time all ingredients are in the drum   4._____
   should be at least 1.5 minutes for a one cubic yard mixer plus 0.5 minutes for each cubic
   yard of capacity over one cubic yard.
   The MINIMUM time to mix 7 cubic yards of concrete is, in minutes,

    A.   3.0   B.   3.5   C.   4.0   D.   4.5

5. It is recommended that a maximum limit be set on mixing time for machine-mixed con-   5._____
   crete because overmixing may remove entrained air and

    A.   increase the water/cement ratio of the mixture
    B.   increase the amount of fine aggregates in the concrete mixture
    C.   the concrete mix may set prematurely
    D.   cause excess water to rise in the placed concrete causing alligator cracks in the
       surface

6.   6._____

Of the following curves, the shape of the roadway section shown above is

    A.   circular   B.   elliptical   C.   parabolic   D.   hyperbolic

7.

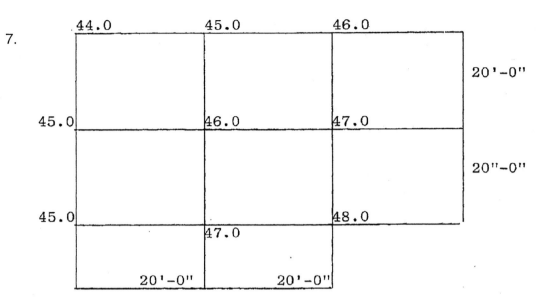

Shown above are the elevations of a borrow pit. The final elevation of the borrow pit after removing the soil is 40.0. Neglecting earth removal outside the borrow pit area, the volume of earth removed is, in cubic yards, MOST NEARLY

A.   347   B.   352   C.   357   D.   362

8.   The shaded area is, in square inches, MOST NEARLY

   A.   18.3
   B.   19.1
   C.   20.0
   D.   20.9

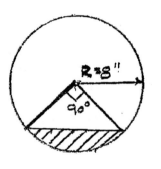

9.   Of the following properties of polymer concrete that make it attractive for maintenance of Portland cement concrete roadways, the one that is MOST important is

   A.   light weight
   B.   immunity to corrosion
   C.   resistance to abrasion
   D.   rapid hardening qualities

10.   A gallon of water weighs MOST NEARLY _____ pounds.

   A.   7.53   B.   8.33   C.   9.13   D.   9.53

11.   Air-entrained concrete is used in concrete roadways primarily to

   A.   reduce the weight of the concrete
   B.   prevent corrosion of the steel reinforcement in the concrete
   C.   make the concrete less porous to the intrusion of water in the concrete
   D.   resist damage to the roadway due to freezing and thawing

12. The slump test in concrete is used to test its   12.____

    A. air content   B. workability
    C. porosity   D. uniformity

13. The criterion for water that is to be used for mixing concrete is that it should be potable.   13.____
This means that the water should

    A. have high turbidity
    B. should be hard
    C. contain no sulfates
    D. be fit for human consumption

14. A test that can be used on an asphalt roadway to measure changes in hardness due to   14.____
age hardening is a _____ test.

    A. ductility
    B. viscosity
    C. ring and ball softening point
    D. penetration

15. A densely graded bituminous mixture is called a large stone mix if the nominal size of   15.____
aggregates is equal to or greater than a minimum of

    A. 1 inch   B. 1 1/4 inches
    C. 1 1/2 inches   D. 1 3/4 inches

16. The specifications state that the surface on which the bituminous material is applied must   16.____
have a temperature of 20°C or higher.
20°C is, in degrees Fahrenheit,

    A. 62°   B. 64°   C. 66°   D. 68°

17. The largest size aggregate in sheet asphalt is usually   17.____

    A. 1/8 inch   B. 1/4 inch   C. 3/8 inch   D. 1/2 inch

18. Sheet asphalt is used mainly in   18.____

    A. rural areas   B. major highways
    C. overpasses   D. city streets

19. Of the following, a slurry seal is NOT used on a bituminous pavement to   19.____

    A. fill potholes
    B. fill cracks
    C. repair raveling asphalt pavement
    D. provide a skid-resistant surface

20. Pozzolan is a *siliceous* material. Another example of a siliceous material is   20.____

    A. clay   B. limestone   C. granite   D. sand

21. The primary purpose of a tack coat that precedes the application of a bitumimous mix on
    an existing surface is to

    A.   remove dust from the existing surface
    B.   fill in cracks in the existing surface
    C.   allow the new mixture to adhere to the existing surface
    D.   prevent the asphalt in the bituminous paving material from seeping into the existing
        pavement

21.____

22. The lowest temperature at which asphalt pavements should be laid is

    A. 30°F   B. 40°F   C. 50°F   D. 60°F?

22.____

23. Steam will rise from an asphalt mix when it is dumped into the hopper of a paver if

    A.   there is too little asphalt in the mix
    B.   excess moisture is present in the mix
    C.   the mix is too hot
    D.   there is an excess of asphalt in the mix

23.____

24. The number of millimeters in an inch is MOST NEARLY

    A. 20   B. 25   C. 30   D. 35

24.____

25. The number of inches in a meter is MOST NEARLY

    A. 39.37   B. 39.57   C. 39.77   D. 39.97

25.____

_____

KEY (CORRECT ANSWERS)

1.	A		11.	D
2.	C		12.	B
3.	A		13.	D
4.	D		14.	D
5.	B		15.	A
6.	C		16.	D
7.	B		17.	B
8.	A		18.	D
9.	D		19.	A
10.	B		20.	D

21.	C
22.	B
23.	B
24.	B
25.	A

_____

TEST 2

DIRECTIONS: Each question or incomplete statement is followed by several suggested answers or completions. Select the one that BEST answers the question or completes the statement. *PRINT THE LETTER OF THE CORRECT ANSWER IN THE SPACE AT THE RIGHT.*

1. Overheated asphalt can often be identified from the _____ in the truck.　　　　1._____

    A.　rich black appearance and the tendency to slump
    B.　slump and leveling out
    C.　blue smoke rising from the mix
    D.　lean, granular appearance of the mix

2. Of the following, the traffic sign shown at the right indi-　　　　2._____
cates a
    A.　school crossing
    B.　no passing zone
    C.　railroad crossing
    D.　deer crossing

3. 90 kilometers per hour is MOST NEARLY _____ miles per hour.　　　　3._____

    A.　40　　　　　　B.　45　　　　　　C.　50　　　　　　D.　55

4. One kilometer is equal to _____ miles.　　　　4._____

    A.　0.5　　　　　B.　0.6　　　　　C.　0.7　　　　　D.　0.8

5. Steel weighs 490 pounds per cubic foot. A one inch square bar of steel one foot long　　　　5._____
weighs MOST NEARLY _____ pounds.

    A.　3.0　　　　　B.　3.4　　　　　C.　3.8　　　　　D.　4.2

6. The size of the fillet weld is dimension　　　　6._____
    A.　A
    B.　B
    C.　C
    D.　D

7. In mowing planted and natural grass adjacent to a roadway, the preferable period is　　　　7._____

    A.　winter　　　　B.　spring　　　　C.　summer　　　　D.　fall

8. Pumping of a roadway surface occurs on   8.____

    A. bituminous pavements only
    B. bituminous and concrete pavements
    C. concrete pavements only
    D. concrete pavements only if they are not air-entrained

9. Pumping of a roadway surface is associated with soils in the subgrade that are   9.____

    A. gravelly
    B. fine grained
    C. coarse grained
    D. distributed in size from fine grained soils to coarse grained soils

10. The buckling or blowup of old concrete pavements is due primarily to the   10.____

    A. failure of longitudinal and transverse joints to function properly
    B. pounding by trucks that the pavement was not designed to carry
    C. failure of the subgrade to transfer the loads upon it
    D. subsurface water that is not drained from beneath the pavement

11. The MOST common type of construction equipment used for clearing and grubbing   11.____
activities is a bulldozer. Bulldozer size is determined by

    A. tread area   B. blade size
    C. drawbar pull   D. flywheel horsepower

12. Sheepsfoot rollers are BEST used to compact   12.____

    A. clay soils   B. sandy soils
    C. gravelly soils   D. graded sand and gravel mix

13. A smooth-wheeled steel roller that is typically water ballasted are most effective on   13.____

    A. granular material such as sand and gravel
    B. clayed material
    C. mixtures of silt, sand and clay
    D. mixtures of sand and clay

14. Of the following machines, the one that would be MOST suitable for grading and shaping   14.____
surfaces, ditching and bank sloping would be a

    A. bulldozer   B. motor grader
    C. front end loader   D. backhoe

15. Supercompactors which are useful for all types of soils weigh from _____ tons.   15.____

    A. 10 to 40   B. 20 to 50   C. 30 to 60   D. 40 to 70

16. A basic objective of the Critical Path Method used on a highway construction project   16.____
would be to

    A. achieve economies in the use of material
    B. achieve economies in the use of equipment
    C. improve the quality of construction
    D. prevent the creation of bottlenecks

17. In the Critical Path Method, free float is the amount of time   17._____

    A. an activity requires to be completed
    B. an activity can be delayed without causing a delay in the succeeding activity
    C. an activity takes to make up for the time lag in the following activity
    D. needed to make up for lost time in a preceding activity

18. Another name for the bar chart used in construction planning and scheduling is the   18._____
    _____ chart.

    A. Fischer   B. Schiff   C. Banff   D. Gantt

19. Of the following, the machine that would LEAST likely be used to excavate large volumes   19._____
    of earth is a

    A. scraper   B. front end loader
    C. shovel   D. clamshell

20. Roadside maintenance generally includes the area between the   20._____

    A. traveled surface and the limits of the right of way
    B. distance between the outer edges of the shoulders on opposite sides of the high-
       way
    C. median strip of the highway
    D. distance between the right of way on opposite sides of the highway

21. The sewer that usually has the greatest depth below grade is usually a(n)_____ sewer.   21._____

    A. sanitary   B. combined
    C. intercepting   D. relieving

22. A combined sewer is a sewer that   22._____

    A. carries storm water and salty water
    B. is made of steel and lined on the inside with concrete
    C. sometimes flow less than full and sometimes is under pressure
    D. carries sewage and storm water

23. If the grade of a sewer is 0.5%, the change in the elevation of the invert of the sewer in   23._____
    350 feet is, in feet and inches,

    A. 1'-9"   B. 1'-10"   C. 1'-11"   D. 2'-0"

24. The National Joint Committee has adopted a color code for traffic control devices. The   24._____
    color brown is used for

    A. direction guidance
    B. general warning
    C. motorist service guidance
    D. public recreation and scenic guidance

25. Of the following, the isosceles traffic sign shown at the right indicates a
    A. traffic separation
    B. no U turn
    C. narrow median-urban
    D. no passing zone

25.____

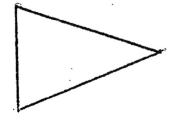

———

KEY (CORRECT ANSWERS)

1.	C		11.	D
2.	A		12.	A
3.	D		13.	A
4.	B		14.	B
5.	B		15.	B
6.	A		16.	D
7.	D		17.	B
8.	C		18.	D
9.	B		19.	D
10.	A		20.	A

21.	C
22.	D
23.	A
24.	D
25.	D

———

EXAMINATION SECTION
TEST 1

DIRECTIONS: Each question or incomplete statement is followed by several suggested answers or completions. Select the one that BEST answers the question or completes the statement. *PRINT THE LETTER OF THE CORRECT ANSWER IN THE SPACE AT THE RIGHT.*

1. Reflective cracks in asphalt overlays

    1.____

  A. are cracks in asphalt overlays that show the crack pattern of the pavement underneath
  B. are cracks that reflect caused by weakness in the base soil
  C. are the result of change in weights and frequency of truck travel in that they are greater than the loads the pavement was designed for
  D. reflect the type of cracks that normally could be expected for this type of pavement

2. In a guide for the estimation of Pavement Condition Rating for asphalt concrete pavement on a highway is the following classification: *Pavement is in fairly good condition with frequent slight cracking or very slight channeling and a few areas with slight alligatoring. Rideability is fairly good with intermittent rough and uneven sections.* The maintenance recommendation for this class of pavement condition is

    2.____

  A. no maintenance required
  B. normal maintenance only
  C. resurface in 3 to 5 years
  D. resurface within 3 years

3. A major problem in bituminous asphalt plants is

    3.____

  A. varying water content in the bituminous aggregate
  B. accuracy in the weighing equipment
  C. air pollution caused by plant exhausts
  D. producing a uniform mixture

4. The primary difference between asphalt concrete and sheet asphalt is asphalt concrete

    4.____

  A. uses a finer sand than sheet asphalt
  B. uses a lower viscosity asphalt than sheet asphalt
  C. generally has a thinner layer than sheet asphalt
  D. contains coarse aggregate whereas sheet asphalt does not have coarse aggregate

5. It is common practice to apply a prime coat over untreated and some treated bases before asphalt concrete is placed. Of the following, the reasons for applying a prime coat are to

    5.____

  A. bind loose particles of the base and minimize heat loss in the applied asphalt concrete
  B. act as a bond between base and pavement and prevent loss of asphalt in the asphalt concrete due to seepage
  C. deter rising moisture from penetrating the pavement and minimize heat loss in the applied asphalt concrete
  D. bind loose particles in the base and deter rising moisture from penetrating the asphalt pavement

6. The asphalt content of open graded mixes is generally at   6.___

    A. the same level as dense graded asphalt
    B. a higher level than dense graded asphalt
    C. a lower level than dense graded asphalt
    D. at a higher or lower level than dense graded asphalt depending on the percent of fine aggregate in the open graded asphalt mix

7. Sheet asphalt was extensively used in the past with a thickness of _____ inch(es).   7.___

    A. 1/2   B. 3/4   C. 1   D. 1 1/2

8. The progressive separation of aggregate particles in a pavement from the surface downward or from the edges inward in an asphalt concrete pavement is known as   8.___

    A. raveling   B. spalling
    C. scaling   D. reflective cracks

9. A profilometer used on an asphalt concrete road measures the _____ the road.   9.___

    A. grade of   B. roughness of
    C. impact resistance of   D. channels in

10. Reinforcing steel is used in a footing. The minimum distance the bottom of the steel is above the subgrade should be _____ inch(es).   10.___

    A. 1   B. 2   C. 3   D. 4

11. Loose sand weighs 120 pounds per cubic foot and the specific gravity of sand is 2.65. The absolute volume of a cubic foot of loose sand is, in cubic feet, most nearly   11.___

    A. .73   B. .75   C. .77   D. .79

12. The maximum size of coarse aggregate in a concrete mix for a reinforced concrete structure is determined by the size of the concrete section and the   12.___

    A. type of cement used
    B. proportion of fine aggregate
    C. minimum distance between reinforcing bars
    D. yield point of the reinforcing steel

13. Cement (High Early Strength) is Type _____ cement.   13.___

    A. I   B. II   C. III   D. IV

14. Slunp in concrete is a measure of   14.___

    A. strength   B. porosity
    C. permeability   D. workability

15. The cross section area of a #8 bar is _____ square inches.   15.___

    A. .60   B. .79   C. 1.00   D. 1.25

16. Construction joints for slabs in a building shall be made   16.____

    A. at the supports
    B. within 1/8 of the span of the slab from the supports
    C. from 1/8 to 3/8 of the span of the slab from the supports
    D. near the center of the span

17. Chutes for depositing concrete shall have a slope no greater than   17.____

A. (triangle with base 1, height 1)   B. (triangle with base 1½, height 1)   C. (triangle with base 2, height 1)   D. (triangle with base 2½, height 1)

18. Air entrained cement is used in a concrete mix on highways primarily to   18.____

    A. make the concrete stronger after 28 days
    B. have a higher early strength
    C. make the surface more resistant to freezing and thawing
    D. make the surface less porous to better resist the impact of trucks

19. Beach sand is unsuitable as a fine aggregate in concrete because it has salt contamination and the sand particles are   19.____

    A. smooth   B. rough
    C. uniform in size   D. too fine

20. The fineness modulus of sand for concrete is taken on the job to insure   20.____

    A. the quality of the sand
    B. that the gradation of the sand does not change
    C. that there is not an excess of fines in the sand
    D. that there is not an excess of oversized particles in the sand

21. The coarse and fine aggregate for concrete are usually tested   21.____

    A. at the quarry site
    B. at the job site
    C. by sampling a loaded truck
    D. in the design engineering office

22. The slump in concrete for highway mixtures range from _____ inches.   22.____

    A. 1 to 3   B. 2 to 5   C. 3 to 6   D. 4 to 7

23. A bag of cement weighs _____ pounds.   23.____

    A. 90   B. 94   C. 97   D. 100

24. The design strength of concrete is to be reached at the end of _____ days.   24.____

    A. 7   B. 14   C. 21   D. 28

25. Of the following, water-cement ratio may be defined as _____ of water per _____ of cement.   25.____

    A. gallons; bag   B. gallons; 100 pounds
    C. quarts; bag   D. quarts; 100 pounds

KEY (CORRECT ANSWERS)

1.	A	11.	A
2.	C	12.	C
3.	C	13.	C
4.	D	14.	D
5.	D	15.	B
6.	B	16.	D
7.	D	17.	C
8.	A	18.	C
9.	B	19.	C
10.	C	20.	B

21.	A
22.	A
23.	B
24.	D
25.	A

————

TEST 2

DIRECTIONS: Each question or incomplete statement is followed by several suggested answers or completions. Select the one that BEST answers the question or completes the statement. *PRINT THE LETTER OF THE CORRECT ANSWER IN THE SPACE AT THE RIGHT.*

1. The maximum size of coarse aggregate in a concrete mix for a reinforced concrete structure is determined by the size of the section and the   1._____

   A. type of cement used
   B. proportion of fine aggregate
   C. minimum distance between reinforcing bars
   D. the yield point of the reinforcing steel

Questions 2-3.

DIRECTIONS: Questions 2 and 3 refer to concrete mix design.

2. The present and most popular method of rational mixture design is sponsored by ACI committee 211, 1994. In this method, the design using ordinary cement is based on   2._____

   A. slump and water-cement ratio
   B. aggregate size and water-cement ratio
   C. slump, aggregate size, and water-cement ratio
   D. slump and water content

3. In the method of mix design of ACI committee 211, 1994, water content is expressed in   3._____

   A. pounds of water per bag of cement
   B. pounds of water per cubic foot of concrete
   C. gallons of water per cubic yard of concrete
   D. pounds of water per cubic yard of concrete

4. The right to use or control the property of another for designated purposes is the definition of   4._____

   A. property acquisition   B. right-of-way
   C. an air right   D. an easement

5. A 24 inch circular drainage pipe is shown on a profile drawing of a highway as an ellipse with the major axis vertical. The reason for this is   5._____

   A. the horizontal and vertical scales of the profile drawing are different
   B. the pipe is not perpendicular to the center line of the roadway
   C. to emphasize the height of the pipe
   D. the slope of the pipe is taken into account

6. On a highway plan is a note for #4 wire game fence reading Lt Sta 2970 + 00 to 2979 + 85, Rt Sta 2970 + 00 to 2980 + 70. The total number of linear feet of new #4 wire game fence is, in feet, most nearly   6._____

   A. 1955   B. 2005   C. 2055   D. 2105

7. The superelevation of a curve is .075 feet. The superelevation, in inches, is most nearly   7._____

    A. 9   B. 5/8   C. 3/4   D. 7/8

8._____

8. On a plan for a highway is a note $\dfrac{\text{S.C.}}{\text{Sta } 2968 + 56.50}$ The S.C. is an abbreviation for

    A. slope at curve   B. spiral to circular curve
    C. superelevated curve   D. separation at center

9. Of the following methods of soil stabilization for the base of a highway pavement, the one   9._____
that is most effective is

    A. a cement admixture
    B. a lime admixture
    C. an emulsified asphalt treated soil
    D. mechanical soil stabilization

10. An asphalt pavement mixture having a brownish dull appearance and lacking a shiny   10._____
black luster

    A. is normal for an asphalt mixture
    B. contains too little aggregate
    C. is too cold
    D. contains too little asphalt

11. Steam rising from an asphalt mix when it is dumped into a hopper indicates   11._____

    A. there is excessive moisture in the aggregate
    B. the mix is overheated
    C. emulsification is taking place
    D. the mixture has not been adequately mixed

12. The disadvantage of excessive fine aggregate in an asphalt mix is   12._____

    A. it is difficult to get a uniform mix
    B. it will require an excessive amount of asphalt
    C. it is difficult to apply because of the grittiness of the mix
    D. the final surface will tend to be rough

13. On highways where heavy trucks are permitted, the percent of total traffic that are heavy   13._____
trucks is, in percent, MOST NEARLY

    A. 4   B. 11   C. 18   D. 25

14. A single axle 80 kN load is equal to _____ pounds per axle.   14._____

    A. 12,000   B. 14,000   C. 16,000   D. 18,000

15. Normal traffic growth in the United States is _____ percent per year.   15._____

    A. 1-2   B. 3-5   C. 5-7   D. 7-9

16. EAL is an abbreviation for _____ axle load   16._____

    A. equal   B. equivalent
    C. effective   D. estimated

17. A roughometer is a single-wheeled trailer instrumented to measure the roughness of a pavement surface. The measure is in inches per   17._____

    A. foot   B. yard   C. hundred yards   D. mile

18. The Atterberg Limit is a test on   18._____

    A. coarse aggregate   B. asphalt
    C. soil   D. Portland cement

19. Of the following, the one that is a high strength bolt is designated   19._____

    A. A7   B. A36   C. A180   D. A325

20. Construction contracts in a broad sense fall into two categories - fixed price and   20._____

    A. cost-plus   B. fixed price plus overhead and profit
    C. negotiated price   D. arbitrated price

21. A punch list on a construction job is usually made by the inspector   21._____

    A. weekly
    B. monthly
    C. continuously during the last half of the job
    D. near the end of the job

22. When an accident occurs on a construction job in which someone is injured, an accident report is usually made out by the   22._____

    A. insurance carrier   B. contractor
    C. inspector   D. inspector's superior

23. The inspector and the contractor share common goals. The one of the goals listed below that is NOT shared by the contractor and the inspector is   23._____

    A. get a good job done
    B. see that the contractor makes a reasonable profit
    C. get the job done as speedily as possible
    D. have the job done at as low a cost as possible

24. A crack relief layer is placed over an existing Portland cement concrete pavement followed by a well-graded intermediate course, then a dense graded surface course. The crack relief layer consists of an open graded   24._____

    A. mix of 100% crushed material with 25-35% interconnected voids
    B. crushed material heavily compacted with no binder
    C. hot mix made up of 80% crushed material with 20% shredded rubber
    D. dense crushed material with voids filled by asphalt

25. Most of the major work performed on the nation's bridges involves   25._____

    A. painting the bridges
    B. upgrading the bridges to carry heavier loads
    C. replacing the concrete decks
    D. replacing the suspenders on cable supported bridges

KEY (CORRECT ANSWERS)

1. C	11. A
2. C	12. B
3. D	13. B
4. D	14. D
5. A	15. B
6. C	16. B
7. D	17. D
8. B	18. C
9. A	19. D
10. D	20. A

21. D
22. B
23. B
24. A
25. C

———

SAFETY
EXAMINATION SECTION
TEST 1

DIRECTIONS: Each question or incomplete statement is followed by several suggested
answers or completions. Select the one that BEST answers the question or
completes the statement. *PRINT THE LETTER OF THE CORRECT ANSWER
IN THE SPACE AT THE RIGHT.*

1. Employees should be familiar with the rules and regulations governing their jobs MAINLY   1._____
to

    A. eliminate overtime
    B. justify mistakes
    C. pass promotion examinations
    D. perform their duties properly

2. When summoning an ambulance for an injured person, it is MOST important to give the   2._____

    A. name of the injured person
    B. nature of the injuries
    C. cause of the accident
    D. location of the injured person

3. The MOST likely cause of accidents involving minor injuries is   3._____

    A. careless work practices
    B. lack of safety devices
    C. inferior equipment and material
    D. insufficient safety posters

4. In an accident report, the information which may be MOST useful in decreasing the   4._____
recurrence of similar type accidents is the

    A. extent of injuries sustained
    B. time the accident happened
    C. number of people involved
    D. cause of the accident

5. If a co-worker is not breathing after receiving an electric shock but is no longer in contact   5._____
with the electricity, it is MOST important for you to

    A. avoid moving him
    B. wrap the victim in a blanket
    C. force him to take hot liquids
    D. start artificial respiration promptly

6. All of the following are features of a successful safety and health program In the work-   6._____
place EXCEPT

A. management commitment to safety, as demonstrated by their involvement in activities
B. interaction and communication among all workers regarding safety and other job-related matters
C. training practices emphasizing job-safety
D. the option of a life Insurance plan offered by the management

7. If a man on a job has to report an accident to the office by telephone, he should request the name of the person taking the call and also note the time.
The reason for this precaution is to fix responsibility for the

   A. entire handling of the accident thereafter
   B. accuracy of the report
   C. recording of the report
   D. preparation of the final written report

7.____

8. Shoes with sponge rubber soles should NOT be worn in working areas MAINLY because they

   A. are not waterproof
   B. are easily punctured by steel objects
   C. do not keep the feet warm
   D. wear out too quickly

8.____

9. A serious safety hazard occurs when a

   A. hardened steel hammer is used to strike a hardened steel surface
   B. soft iron hammer is used to strike a hardened steel surface
   C. hardened steel hammer is used to strike a soft iron surface
   D. soft iron hammer is used to strike a soft iron surface

9.____

10. When an emergency exit door set in the sidewalk is being opened from inside the subway, the door should be opened slowly to avoid

   A. injury to pedestrian
   B. making unnecessary noise
   C. a sudden rush of air from the street
   D. damage to the sidewalk

10.____

11. The MAIN reason for not permitting more than one person to work on a ladder at the same time is that

   A. the ladder might get overloaded
   B. several persons on the ladder might obstruct each other
   C. time would be lost going up and down the ladder
   D. several persons could not all face the ladder at one time

11.____

12. Safety on the job is BEST assured by

   A. keeping alert
   B. working only with new tools
   C. working very slowly
   D. avoiding the necessity for working overtime

12.____

13. An employee will MOST likely avoid accidental injury if he   13.____

    A. stops to rest frequently
    B. works alone
    C. keeps mentally alert
    D. works very slowly

14. The BEST immediate first aid treatment for a scraped knee is to   14.____

    A. apply plain vaseline
    B. use a knee splint
    C. apply heat
    D. wash it with soap and water

15. If, when you are using an extension light with a long cord, the light should go out suddenly, the FIRST thing you should do is to   15.____

    A. inspect the cord for a broken wire
    B. replace the bulb with a new one
    C. check the fuses in the supply circuit
    D. check if the plug is still in the outlet

16. When carrying pipe, employees are cautioned against lifting with the fingers inserted in the ends.
The PROBABLE reason for this caution is to avoid the possibility of   16.____

    A. dropping and damaging pipe
    B. getting dirt and perspiration on inside of pipe
    C. cutting the fingers on edge of pipe
    D. straining finger muscles

17. Artificial respiration after a severe electric shock is ALWAYS necessary when the shock results in   17.____

    A. unconsciousness   B. stoppage of breathing
    C. bleeding   D. a burn

18. The MOST common cause for a workman to lose his balance and fall when working from an extension ladder is   18.____

    A. too much spring in the ladder
    B. sideways sliding of the top
    C. exerting a heavy pull on an object which gives suddenly
    D. working on something directly behind the ladder

19. It is NOT necessary to wear protective goggles when   19.____

    A. drilling rivet holes in a steel beam
    B. sharpening tools on a power grinder
    C. welding a steel plate to a pipe column
    D. laying up a cinder block partition

20. The Department gives some of its maintenance employees instruction in first aid. 20.___
The MOST likely reason for doing this is to

    A. eliminate the need for calling a doctor in case of accident
    B. reduce the number of accidents
    C. lower the cost of accidents to the Department
    D. provide temporary emergency treatment in case of accident

21. The BEST immediate first aid if a chemical solution splashes into the eyes is to 21.___

    A. protect the eyes from the light by bandaging
    B. flush the eyes with large quantities of clean water
    C. cause tears to flow by staring at a bright light
    D. rub the eyes dry with a towel

22. It is IMPORTANT to make certain that a ladle does not contain water before using it to 22.___
scoop up molten solder since the water may

    A. cause serious personal injury
    B. prevent the solder from sticking
    C. cool the solder
    D. dilute the solder

23. If the feet of a ladder are found to be resting on a slightly uneven surface, it would be 23.___
BEST to

    A. move the ladder to an entirely different location
    B. even up the feet of the ladder with a small wedge
    C. get two men to bolster the ladder while it is being climbed
    D. get another ladder that is more suitable to the conditions

24. There are a few workers who are seemingly prone to accidents and who, regardless of 24.___
their assigned job, have a higher accident rate than the average worker.
If your co-worker is known to be such an individual, the BEST course for you to pursue
would be to

    A. do most of the assigned work yourself
    B. refuse to work with this individual
    C. provide him with a copy of all rules and regulations
    D. personally check all safety precautions on each job

25. If a person has a deep puncture in his finger caused by a sharp nail, the BEST immedi- 25.___
ate first aid procedure would be to

    A. prevent air from reaching the wound
    B. stop all bleeding
    C. encourage bleeding by exerting pressure around the injured area
    D. probe the wound for steel particles

KEY (CORRECT ANSWERS)

1.	D	11.	A
2.	D	12.	A
3.	A	13.	C
4.	D	14.	D
5.	D	15.	D
6.	D	16.	C
7.	C	17.	B
8.	B	18.	C
9.	A	19.	D
10.	A	20.	D

21.	B
22.	A
23.	B
24.	D
25.	C

———

TEST 2

DIRECTIONS: Each question or incomplete statement is followed by several suggested answers or completions. Select the one that BEST answers the question or completes the statement. *PRINT THE LETTER OF THE CORRECT ANSWER IN THE SPACE AT THE RIGHT.*

1. An outstanding cause of accidents is the improper use of tools.
   The MOST helpful conclusion you can draw from this statement is that

   A. most tools are defective
   B. many accidents involving the use of tools occur because of poor working habits
   C. most workers are poorly trained
   D. many accidents involving the use of tools are unavoidable

1.____

2. If it is necessary to lift up and hold one heavy part of a piece of equipment with a pinch bar so that there is enough clearance to work with the hands under the part, one IMPORTANT precaution is to

   A. wear gloves
   B. watch the bar to be ready if it slips
   C. work as fast as possible
   D. insert a temporary block to hold the part

2.____

Questions 3-10.

DIRECTIONS: Questions 3 through 10, inclusive, are based on the ladder safety rules given below. Read these rules carefully before answering these items.

LADDER SAFETY RULES

When a ladder is placed on a slightly uneven supporting surface, use a flat piece of board or small wedge to even up the ladder feet. To secure the proper angle for resting a ladder, it should be placed so that the distance from the base of the ladder to the supporting wall is 1/4 the length of the ladder. To avoid overloading a ladder, only one person should work on a ladder at a time. Do not place a ladder in front of a door. When the top rung of a ladder rests against a pole, the ladder should be lashed securely. Clear loose stones or debris from the ground around the base of a ladder before climbing. While on a ladder, do not attempt to lean so that any part of the body, except arms or hands, extends more than 12 inches beyond the side rail. Always face the ladder when ascending or descending. When carrying ladders through buildings, watch for ceiling globes and lighting fixtures. Avoid the use of rolling ladders as scaffold supports.

3. A small wedge is used to

   A. even up the feet of a ladder resting on an uneven surface
   B. lock the wheels of a roller ladder
   C. secure the proper resting angle for a ladder
   D. secure a ladder against a pole

3.____

4. An 8 foot ladder resting against a wall should be so inclined that the distance between the base of the ladder and the wall is _____ feet.

    A. 2   B. 5   C. 7   D. 9

    4.____

5. A ladder should be lashed securely when

    A. it is placed in front of a door
    B. loose stones are on the ground near the base of the ladder
    C. the top rung rests against a pole
    D. two people are working from the same ladder

    5.____

6. Rolling ladders

    A. should be used for scaffold supports
    B. should not be used for scaffold supports
    C. are useful on uneven ground
    D. should be used against a pole

    6.____

7. When carrying a ladder through a building, it is necessary to

    A. have two men to carry it
    B. carry the ladder vertically
    C. watch for ceiling globes
    D. face the ladder while carrying it

    7.____

8. It is POOR practice to

    A. lash a ladder securely at any time
    B. clear debris from the base of a ladder before climbing
    C. even up the feet of a ladder resting on slightly uneven ground
    D. place a ladder in front of a door

    8.____

9. A person on a ladder should NOT extend his head beyond the side rail by more than _____ inches.

    A. 12   B. 9   C. 7   D. 5

    9.____

10. The MOST important reason for permitting only one person to work on a ladder at a time is that

    A. both could not face the ladder at one time
    B. the ladder would be overloaded
    C. time would be lost going up and down the ladder
    D. they would obstruct each othe

    10.____

11. The MOST important reason for roping off a work area on a subway station is to

    A. protect the public
    B. protect the repair crew
    C. prevent distraction of the crew by the public
    D. prevent delays to the public

    11.____

12. Fire extinguishers and other fire safety equipment should be inspected   12.____

    A. only when they are malfunctioning
    B. at regular intervals
    C. when there is danger of a fire
    D. during the summer

13. It is POOR practice to hold a piece of wood in the hands or lap when tightening a screw   13.____
in the wood because

    A. sufficient leverage cannot be obtained
    B. the screwdriver may bend
    C. the wood will probably split
    D. personal injury is likely to result

14. Steel helmets give workers the MOST protection from   14.____

    A. falling objects   B. eye injuries
    C. fire   D. electric shock

15. It is POOR practice to wear goggles when   15.____

    A. chipping stone
    B. using a grinder
    C. climbing or descending ladders
    D. handling molten metal

16. When using a brace and bit to bore a hole completely through a partition, it is MOST   16.____
important to

    A. lean heavily on the brace and bit
    B. maintain a steady turning speed all through the job
    C. have the body in a position that will not be easily thrown off balance
    D. reverse the direction of the bit at frequent intervals

17. Gloves should be used when handling   17.____

    A. lanterns   B. wooden rules
    C. heavy ropes   D. all small tools

18. If a fellow worker has stopped breathing after an electric shock, the BEST first aid treat-   18.____
ment is

    A. artificial respiration
    B. to massage his chest
    C. an application of cold compresses
    D. a hot drink

19. Tools used in maintenance work should ALWAYS be kept in good condition because   19.____

    A. a good job can never be done without perfect tools
    B. tools that are in good condition require no care
    C. defective tools may cause accidents or damage
    D. good tools are less easily lost

20. When the foot of an extension ladder, placed against a high wall, rests on a sidewalk or another such similar surface, it is advisable to tie a rope between the bottom rung of the ladder and a point on the wall opposite this rung.
This is done to prevent

    A. people from walking under the ladder
    B. another worker from removing the ladder
    C. the ladder from vibrating when ascending or descending
    D. the foot of the ladder from slipping

20.____

21. In construction work, ALMOST ALL accidents can be blamed on the

    A. failure of an individual to give close attention to the job assigned to him
    B. use of improper tools
    C. lack of cooperation among the men in a gang
    D. fact that an incompetent man was placed in a key position

21.____

22. If it is necessary for you to do some work with your hands under a piece of heavy equipment, while a fellow worker lifts up and holds one end of it by means of a pinch bar, one IMPORTANT precaution you should take is to

    A. wear gloves
    B. watch the bar to be ready if it slips
    C. insert a temporary block to support the piece
    D. work as fast as possible

22.____

23. Protective goggles should NOT be worn when

    A. standing on a ladder drilling a steel beam
    B. descending a ladder after completing a job
    C. chipping concrete near a third rail
    D. sharpening a cold chisel on a grinding stone

23.____

24. In preparing to raise a steel beam to position during steel erection, the man placing the slings puts only one sling near the center of the beam rather than a sling at each end.
This procedure is

    A. *poor* because of the possibility of the beam slipping through the one sling
    B. *good* because it allows the beam to be tilted at the ends for necessary maneuvering
    C. *poor* because the safeguards against sling breakage is cut in half
    D. *good* because the one sling can be placed faster than the two

24.____

25. Which of the following would provide the LEAST effective response to a health, hazard in the workplace after an accident has occurred?

    A. Change the system in order to eliminate the hazard
    B. Control the hazard by enclosing or guarding it
    C. Train employees in safe job procedures to increase their awareness
    D. Ignoring this accident and planning to act if another similar one occurs

25.____

KEY (CORRECT ANSWERS)

1.	B	11.	A
2.	D	12.	B
3.	A	13.	D
4.	A	14.	A
5.	C	15.	C
6.	B	16.	C
7.	C	17.	C
8.	D	18.	A
9.	A	19.	C
10.	B	20.	D

21.	A
22.	C
23.	B
24.	A/B
25.	D

_____

EXAMINATION SECTION
TEST 1

DIRECTIONS: Each question or incomplete statement is foll'owed by several suggested answers or completions. Select the one that BEST answers the question or completes the statement. *PRINT THE LETTER OF THE CORRECT ANSWER IN THE SPACE AT THE RIGHT.*

1. Of the following, the one MOST important quality required of a good supervisor is   1.____

   A. ambition
   C. friendliness
   B. leadership
   D. popularity

2. It is often said that a supervisor can delegate authority but never responsibility. This means MOST NEARLY that   2.____

   A. a supervisor must do his own work if he expects it to be done properly
   B. a supervisor can assign someone else to do his work, but in the last analysis, the supervisor himself must take the blame for any actions followed
   C. authority and responsibility are two separate things that cannot be borne by the same person
   D. it is better for a supervisor never to delegate his authority

3. One of your men who is a habitual complainer asks you to grant him a minor privilege. Before granting or denying such a request, you should consider   3.____

   A. the merits of the case
   B. that it is good for group morale to grant a request of this nature
   C. the man's seniority
   D. that to deny such a request will lower your standing with the men

4. A supervisory practice on the part of a foreman which is MOST likely to lead to confusion and inefficiency is for him to   4.____

   A. give orders verbally directly to the man assigned to the job
   B. issue orders only in writing
   C. follow up his orders after issuing them
   D. relay his orders to the men through co-workers

5. It would be POOR supervision on a foreman's part if he   5.____

   A. asked an experienced maintainer for his opinion on the method of doing a special job
   B. make it a policy to avoid criticizing a man in front of his co-workers
   C. consulted his assistant supervisor on unusual problems
   D. allowed a cooling-off period of several days before giving one of his men a deserved reprimand

6. Of the following behavior characteristics of a supervisor, the one that is MOST likely to lower the morale of the men he supervises is   6.____

   A. diligence
   C. punctuality
   B. favoritism
   D. thoroughness

7. Of the following, the BEST method of getting an employee who is not working up to his capacity to produce more work is to   7.____

    A. have another employee criticize his production
    B. privately criticize his production but encourage him to produce more
    C. criticize his production before his associates
    D. criticize his production and threaten to fire him

8. Of the following, the BEST thing for a supervisor to do when a subordinate has done a very good job is to   8.____

    A. tell him to take it easy
    B. praise his work
    C. reduce his workload
    D. say nothing because he may become conceited

9. Your orders to your crew are MOST likely to be followed if you   9.____

    A. explain the reasons for these orders
    B. warn that all violators will be punished
    C. promise easy assignments to those who follow these orders best
    D. say that they are for the good of the department

10. In order to be a good supervisor, you should   10.____

    A. impress upon your men that you demand perfection in their work at all times
    B. avoid being blamed for your crew's mistakes
    C. impress your superior with your ability
    D. see to it that your men get what they are entitled to

11. In giving instructions to a crew, you should   11.____

    A. speak in as loud a tone as possible
    B. speak in a coaxing, persuasive manner
    C. speak quietly, clearly, and courteously
    D. always use the word *please* when giving instructions

12. Of the following factors, the one which is LEAST important in evaluating an employee and his work is his   12.____

    A. dependability   B. quantity of work done
    C. quality of work done   D. education and training

13. When a District Superintendent first assumes his command, it is LEAST important for him at the beginning to observe   13.____

    A. how his equipment is designed and its adaptability
    B. how to reorganize the district for greater efficiency
    C. the capabilities of the men in the district
    D. the methods of operation being employed

14. When making an inspection of one of the buildings under your supervision, the BEST   14.____
procedure to follow in making a record of the inspection is to

    A. return immediately to the office and write a report from memory
    B. write down all the important facts during or as soon as you complete the inspection
    C. fix in your mind all important facts so that you can repeat them from memory if necessary
    D. fix in your mind all important facts so that you can make out your report at the end of the day

15. Assume that your superior has directed you to make certain changes in your established   15.____
procedure. After using this modified procedure on several occasions, you find that the
original procedure was distinctly superior and you wish to return to it.
You should

    A. let your superior find this out for himself
    B. simply change back to the original procedure
    C. compile definite data and information to prove your case to your superior
    D. persuade one of the more experienced workers to take this matter up with your superior

16. An inspector visited a large building under construction. He inspected the soil lines at 9   16.____
M., water lines at 10 A.M., fixtures at 11 A.M., and did his office work in the afternoon. He
followed the same pattern daily for weeks.
This procedure was

    A. *good;* because it was methodical and he did not miss anything
    B. *good;* because it gave equal time to all phases of the plumbing
    C. *bad;* because not enough time was devoted to fixtures
    D. *bad;* because the tradesmen knew when the inspection would occur

17. Assume that one of the foremen in a training course, which you are conducting, pro-   17.____
poses a poor solution for a maintenance problem.
Of the following, the BEST course of action for you to take is to

    A. accept the solution tentatively and correct it during the next class meeting
    B. point out all the defects of this proposed solution and wait until somebody thinks of a better solution
    C. try to get the class to reject this proposed solution and develop a better solution
    D. let the matter pass since somebody will present a better solution as the class work proceeds

18. As a supervisor, you should be seeking ways to improve the efficiency of shop operations   18.____
by means such as changing established work procedures.
The following are offered as possible actions that you should consider in changing
established work procedures:
    I. Make changes only when your foremen agree to them
    II. Discuss changes with your supervisor before putting them into practice
    III. Standardize any operation which is performed on a continuing basis
    IV. Make changes quickly and quietly in order to avoid dissent
    V. Secure expert guidance before instituting unfamiliar procedures

Of the following suggested answers, the one that describes the actions to be taken to change established work procedures is

A. I, IV, and V *only*
B. II, III, and V *only*
C. III, IV, and V *only*
D. All of the above

19. A supervisor determined that a foreman, without informing his superior, delegated responsibility for checking time cards to a member of his gang. The supervisor then called the foreman into his office where he reprimanded the foreman.
This action of the supervisor in reprimanding the foreman was

A. *proper*; because the checking of time cards is the foreman's responsibility and should not be delegated
B. proper; because the foreman did not ask the supervisor for permission to delegate responsibility
C. improper; because the foreman may no longer take the initiative in solving future problems
D. *improper*; because the supervisor is interfering in a function which is not his responsibility

19.____

20. A capable supervisor should check all operations under his control.
Of the following, the LEAST important reason for doing this is to make sure that

A. operations are being performed as scheduled
B. he personally observes all operations at all times
C. all the operations are still needed
D. his manpower is being utilized efficiently

20.____

21. A supervisor makes it a practice to apply fair and firm discipline in all cases of rule infractions, including those of a minor nature.
This practice should PRIMARILY be considered

A. *bad;* since applying discipline for minor violations is a waste of time
B. *good;* because not applying discipline for minor infractions can lead to a more serious erosion of discipline
C. *bad*; because employees do not like to be disciplined for minor violations of the rules
D. *good;* because violating any rule can cause a dangerous situation to occur

21.____

22. A maintainer would PROPERLY consider it poor supervisory practice for a foreman to consult with him on

A. which of several repair jobs should be scheduled first
B. how to cope with personal problems at home
C. whether the neatness of his headquarters can be improved
D. how to express a suggestion which the maintainer plans to submit formally

22.____

23. Assume that you have determined that the work of one of your foremen and the men he supervises is consistently behind schedule. When you discuss this situation with the foreman, he tells you that his men are poor workers and then complains that he must spend all of his time checking on their work.

    The following actions are offered for your consideration as possible ways of solving the problem of poor performance of the foreman and his men:

      I.   Review the work standards with the foreman and determine whether they are realistic

      II.   Tell the foreman that you will recommend him for the foreman's training course for retraining

      III.   Ask the foreman for the names of the maintainers and then replace them as soon as possible

      IV.   Tell the foreman that you expect him to meet a satisfactory level of performance

      V.   Tell the foreman to insist that his men work overtime to catch up to the schedule

      VI.   Tell the foreman to review the type and amount of training he has given the maintainers

      VII.   Tell the foreman that he will be out of a job if he does not produce on schedule

      VIII.   Avoid all criticism of the foreman and his methods

    Which of the following suggested answers CORRECTLY lists the proper actions to be taken to solve the problem of poor performance of the foreman and his men?

    A.   I, II, IV, and VI *only*
    B.   I, III, V, and VII *only*
    C.   II, III, VI, and VIII *only*
    D.   IV, V, VI, and VIII *only*

24. When a conference or a group discussion is tending to turn into a *bull session* without constructive purpose, the BEST action to take is to

    A.   reprimand the leader of the *bull session*
    B.   redirect the discussion to the business at hand
    C.   dismiss the meeting and reschedule it for another day
    D.   allow the *bull session* to continue

25. Assume that you have been assigned responsibility for a program in which a high production rate is mandatory. From past experience, you know that your foremen do not perform equally well in the various types of jobs given to them.

    Which of the following methods should you use in selecting foremen for the specific types of work involved in the program?

    A.   Leave the method of selecting foremen to your supervisor
    B.   Assign each foreman to the work he does best
    C.   Allow each foreman to choose his own job
    D.   Assign each foreman to a job which will permit him to improve his own abilities

KEY (CORRECT ANSWERS)

1.	B		11.	C
2.	B		12.	D
3.	A		13.	B
4.	D		14.	B
5.	D		15.	C
6.	B		16.	D
7.	B		17.	C
8.	B		18.	B
9.	A		19.	A
10.	D		20.	B

21.	B
22.	A
23.	A
24.	B
25.	B

———

TEST 2

DIRECTIONS: Each question or incomplete statement is followed by several suggested answers or completions. Select the one that BEST answers the question or completes the statement. *PRINT THE LETTER OF THE CORRECT ANSWER IN THE SPACE AT THE RIGHT.*

1. A foreman who is familiar with modern management principles should know that the one of the following requirements of an administrator which is LEAST important is his ability to

    A. coordinate work
    B. plan, organize, and direct the work under his control
    C. cooperate with others
    D. perform the duties of the employees under his jurisdiction

1._____

2. When subordinates request his advice in solving problems encountered in their work, a certain chief occasionally answers the request by first asking the subordinate what he thinks should be done.
This action by the chief is, on the whole,

    A. *desirable* because it stimulates subordinates to give more thought to the solution of problems encountered
    B. *undesirable* because it discourages subordinates from asking questions
    C. *desirable* because it discourages subordinates from asking questions
    D. *undesirable* because it undermines the confidence of subordinates in the ability of their supervisor

2._____

3. Of the following factors that may be considered by a unit head in dealing with the tardy subordinate, the one which should be given LEAST consideration is the

    A. frequency with which the employee is tardy
    B. effect of the employee's tardiness upon the work of other employees
    C. willingness of the employee to work overtime when necessary
    D. cause of the employee's tardiness

3._____

4. The MOST important requirement of a good inspectional report is that it should be

    A. properly addressed   B. lengthy
    C. clear and brief   D. spelled correctly

4._____

5. Building superintendents frequently inquire about departmental inspectional procedures. Of the following, it is BEST to

    A. advise them to write to the department for an official reply
    B. refuse as the inspectional procedure is a restricted matter
    C. briefly explain the procedure to them
    D. avoid the inquiry by changing the subject

5._____

6. Reprimanding a crew member before other workers is a

    A. *good practice;* the reprimand serves as a warning to the other workers
    B. *bad practice;* people usually resent criticism made in public
    C. *good practice;* the other workers will realize that the supervisor is fair
    D. *bad practice;* the other workers will take sides in the dispute

6._____

7. Of the following actions, the one which is LEAST likely to promote good work is for the group leader to 7.____

    A. praise workers for doing a good job
    B. call attention to the opportunities for promotion for better workers
    C. threaten to recommend discharge of workers who are below standard
    D. put into practice any good suggestion made by crew members

8. A supervisor notices that a member of his crew has skipped a routine step in his job. Of the following, the BEST action for the supervisor to take is to 8.____

    A. promptly question the worker about the incident
    B. immediately assign another man to complete the job
    C. bring up the incident the next time the worker asks for a favor
    D. say nothing about the incident but watch the worker carefully in the future

9. Assume you have been told to show a new worker how to operate a piece of equipment. Your FIRST step should be to 9.____

    A. ask the worker if he has any questions about the equipment
    B. permit the worker to operate the equipment himself while you carefully watch to prevent damage
    C. demonstrate the operation of the equipment for the worker
    D. have the worker read an instruction booklet on the maintenance of the equipment

10. Whenever a new man was assigned to his crew, the supervisor would introduce him to all other crew members, take him on a tour of the plant, tell him about bus schedules and places to eat.
This practice is 10.____

    A. *good;* the new man is made to feel welcome
    B. *bad;* supervisors should not interfere in personal matters
    C. *good;* the new man knows that he can bring his personal problems to the supervisor
    D. *bad;* work time should not be spent on personal matters

11. The MOST important factor in successful leadership is the ability to 11.____

    A. obtain instant obedience to all orders
    B. establish friendly personal relations with crew members
    C. avoid disciplining crew members
    D. make crew members want to do what should be done

12. Explaining the reasons for departmental procedure to workers tends to 12.____

    A. waste time which should be used for productive purposes
    B. increase their interest in their work
    C. make them more critical of departmental procedures
    D. confuse them

13. If you want a job done well, do it yourself. For a supervisor to follow this advice would be   13.____

    A. *good;* a supervisor is responsible for the work of his crew
    B. *bad;* a supervisor should train his men, not do their work
    C. *good;* a supervisor should be skilled in all jobs assigned to his crew
    D. *bad;* a supervisor loses respect when he works with his hands

14. When a supervisor discovers a mistake in one of the jobs for which his crew is responsible, it is MOST important for him to find out   14.____

    A. whether anybody else knows about the mistake
    B. who was to blame for the mistake
    C. how to prevent similar mistakes in the future
    D. whether similar mistakes occurred in the past

15. A supervisor who has to explain a new procedure to his crew should realize that questions from the crew USUALLY show that they   15.____

    A. are opposed to the new procedure
    B. are completely confused by the explanation
    C. need more training in the new procedure
    D. are interested in the explanation

16. A good way for a supervisor to retain the confidence of his or her employees is to   16.____

    A. say as little as possible
    B. check work frequently
    C. make no promises unless they will be fulfilled
    D. never hesitate in giving an answer to any question

17. Good supervision is ESSENTIALLY a matter of   17.____

    A. patience in supervising workers
    B. care in selecting workers
    C. skill in human relations
    D. fairness in disciplining workers

18. It is MOST important for an employee who has been assigned a monotonous task to   18.____

    A. perform this task before doing other work
    B. ask another employee to help
    C. perform this task only after all other work has been completed
    D. take measures to prevent mistakes in performing the task

19. One of your employees has violated a minor agency regulation .
The FIRST thing you should do is   19.____

    A. warn the employee that you will have to take disciplinary action if it should happen again
    B. ask the employee to explain his or her actions
    C. inform your supervisor and wait for advice
    D. write a memo describing the incident and place it in the employee's personnel file

20. One of your employees tells you that he feels you give him much more work than the   20._____
other employees, and he is having trouble meeting your deadlines.
You should

    A. ask if he has been under a lot of non-work related stress lately
    B. review his recent assignments to determine if he is correct
    C. explain that this is a busy time, but you are dividing the work equally
    D. tell him that he is the most competent employee and that is why he receives more work

21. A supervisor assigns one of his crew to complete a portion of a job. A short time later, the   21._____
supervisor notices that the portion has not been completed.
Of the following, the BEST way for the supervisor to handle this is to

    A. ask the crew member why he has not completed the assignment
    B. reprimand the crew member for not obeying orders
    C. assign another crew member to complete the assignment
    D. complete the assignment himself

22. Suppose that a member of your crew complains that you are *playing favorites* in assign-   22._____
ing work.
Of the following, the BEST method of handling the complaint is to

    A. deny it and refuse to discuss the matter with the worker
    B. take the opportunity to tell the worker what is wrong with his work
    C. ask the worker for examples to prove his point and try to clear up any misunderstanding
    D. promise to be more careful in making assignments in the future

23. A member of your crew comes to you with a complaint. After discussing the matter with   23._____
him, it is clear that you have convinced him that his complaint was not justified.
At this point, you should

    A. permit him to drop the matter
    B. make him admit his error
    C. pretend to see some justification in his complaint
    D. warn him against making unjustified complaints

24. Suppose that a supervisor has in his crew an older man who works rather slowly. In other   24._____
respects, this man is a good worker; he is seldom absent, works carefully, never loafs,
and is cooperative.
The BEST way for the supervisor to handle this worker is to

    A. try to get him to work faster and less carefully
    B. give him the most disagreeable job
    C. request that he be given special training
    D. permit him to work at his own speed

25. Suppose that a member of your crew comes to you with a suggestion he thinks will save 25.____
time in doing a job. You realize immediately that it won't work.
Under these circumstances, your BEST action would be to

    A. thank the worker for the suggestion and forget about it
    B. explain to the worker why you think it won't work
    C. tell the worker to put the suggestion in writing
    D. ask the other members of your crew to criticize the suggestion

––––––––

KEY (CORRECT ANSWERS)

1.	D		11.	D
2.	A		12.	B
3.	C		13.	B
4.	C		14.	C
5.	C		15.	D
6.	B		16.	C
7.	C		17.	C
8.	A		18.	D
9.	C		19.	B
10.	A		20.	B

21.	A
22.	C
23.	A
24.	D
25.	B

––––––––

SUPERVISION STUDY GUIDE

Social science has developed information about groups and leadership in general and supervisor-employee relationships in particular. Since organizational effectiveness is closely linked to the ability of supervisors to direct the activities of employees, these findings are important to executives everywhere.

IS A SUPERVISOR A LEADER?

First-line supervisors are found in all large business and government organizations. They are the men at the base of an organizational hierarchy. Decisions made by the head of the organization reach them through a network of intermediate positions. They are frequently referred to as part of the management team, but their duties seldom seem to support this description.

A supervisor of clerks, tax collectors, meat inspectors, or securities analysts is not charged with budget preparation. He cannot hire or fire the employees in his own unit on his say-so. He does not administer programs which require great planning, coordinating, or decision making.

Then what is he? He is the man who is directly in charge of a group of employees doing productive work for a business or government agency. If the work requires the use of machines, the men he supervises operate them. If the work requires the writing of reports, the men he supervises write them. He is expected to maintain a productive flow of work without creating problems which higher levels of management must solve. But is he a leader?

To carry out a specific part of an agency's mission, management creates a unit, staffs it with a group of employees and designates a supervisor to take charge of them. Management directs what this unit shall do, from time to time changes directions, and often indicates what the group should not do. Management presumably creates status for the supervisor by giving him more pay, a title, and special priviledges.

Management asks a supervisor to get his workers to attain organizational goals, including the desired quantity and quality of production. Supposedly, he has authority to enable him to achieve this objective. Management at least assumes that by establishing the status of the supervisor's position it has created sufficient authority to enable him to achieve these goals -- not his goals, nor necessarily the group's, but management's goals.

In addition, supervision includes writing reports, keeping records of membership in a higher-level administrative group, industrial engineering, safety engineering, editorial duties, housekeeping duties, etc. The supervisor as a member of an organizational network, must be responsible to the changing demands of the management above him. At the same time, he must be responsive to the demands of the work group of which he is a member. He is placed in the difficult position of communicating and implementing new decisions, changed programs and revised production quotas for his work group, although he may have had little part in developing them.

It follows, then, that supervision has a special characteristic: achievement of goals, previously set by management, through the efforts of others. It is in this feature of the supervisor's job that we find the role of a leader in the sense of the following definition: *A leader is that person who* <u>*most*</u> *effectively influences group activities toward goal setting and goal achievements.*

This definition is broad. It covers both leaders in groups that come together voluntarily and in those brought together through a work assignment in a factory, store, or government agency. In the natural group, the authority necessary to attain goals is determined by the group membership and is granted by them. In the working group, it is apparent that the establishment of a supervisory position creates a predisposition on the part of employees to accept the authority of the occupant of that position. We cannot, however, assume that mere occupancy confers authority sufficient to assure the accomplishment of an organization's goals.

Supervision is different, then, from leadership. The supervisor is expected to fulfill the role of leader but without obtaining a grant of authority from the group he supervises. The supervisor is expected to influence the group in the achieving of goals but is often handicapped by having little influence on the organizational process by which goals are set. The supervisor, because he works in an organizational setting, has the burdens of additional organizational duties and restrictions and requirements arising out of the fact that his position is subordinate to a hierarchy of higher-level supervisors. These differences between leadership and supervision are reflected in our definition: *Supervision is basically a leadership role, in a formal organization, which has as its objective the effective influencing of other employees.*

Even though these differences between supervision and leadership exist, a significant finding of experimenters in this field is that supervisors <u>must</u> be leaders to be successful.

The problem is: How can a supervisor exercise leadership in an organizational setting? We might say that the supervisor is expected to be a natural leader in a situation which does not come about naturally. His situation becomes really difficult in an organization which is more eager to make its supervisors into followers rather than leaders.

LEADERSHIP: NATURAL AND ORGANIZATIONAL

Leadership, in its usual sense of *natural* leadership, and supervision are not the same. In some cases, leadership embraces broader powers and functions than supervision; in other cases, supervision embraces more than leadership. This is true both because of the organization and technical aspects of the supervisor's job and because of the relatively freer setting and inherent authority of the natural leader.

The natural leader usually has much more authority and influence than the supervisor. Group members not only follow his command but prefer it that way. The employee, however, can appeal the supervisor's commands to his union or to the supervisor's superior or to the personnel office. These intercessors represent restrictions on the supervisor's power to lead.

The natural leader can gain greater membership involvement in the group's objectives, and he can change the objectives of the group. The supervisor can attempt to gain employee support only for management's objectives; he cannot set other objectives. In these instances leadership is broader than supervision.

The natural leader must depend upon whatever skills are available when seeking to attain objectives. The supervisor is trained in the administrative skills necessary to achieve management's goals. If he does not possess the requisite skills, however, he can call upon management's technicians.

A natural leader can maintain his leadership, in certain groups, merely by satisfying members' need for group affilation. The supervisor must maintain his leadership by directing and organizing his group to achieve specific organizational goals set for him and his group by management. He must have a technical competence and a kind of coordinating ability which is not needed by many natural leaders.

A natural leader is responsible only to his group which grants him authority. The supervisor is responsible to management, which employs him, and, also, to the work group of which he is a member. The supervisor has the exceedingly difficult job of reconciling the demands of two groups frequently in conflict. He is often placed in the untenable position of trying to play two antagonisic roles. In the above instances, supervision is broader than leadership.

ORGANIZATIONAL INFLUENCES ON LEADERSHIP

The supervisor is both a product and a prisoner of the organization wherein we find him. The organization which creates the supervisor's position also obstructs, restricts, and channelizes the exercise of his duties. These influences extend beyond prescribed functional relationships to specific supervisory behavior. For example, even in a face-to-face situation involving one of his subordinates, the supervisor's actions are controlled to a great extent by his organization. His behavior must conform to the organization policy on human relations, rules which dictate personnel procedures, specific prohibitions governing conduct, the attitudes of his own superior, etc. He is not a free agent operating within the limits of his work group. His freedom of action is much more circumscribed than is generally admitted. The organizational influences which limit his leadership actions can be classified as structure, prescriptions, and proscriptions.

The organizational structure places each supervisor's position in context with other designated positions. It determines the relationships between his position and specific positions which impinge on his. The structure of the organization designates a certain position to which he looks for orders and information about his work. It gives a particular status to his position within a pattern of statuses from which he perceives that (1) certain positions are on a par, organizationally, with his, (2) other positions are subordinate, and (3) still others are superior. The organizational structure determines those positions to which he should look for advice and assistance, and those positions to which he should give advice and assistance.

For instance, the organizational structure has predetermined that the supervisor of a clerical processing unit shall report to a supervisory position in a higher echelon. He shall have certain relationships with the supervisors of the work units which transmit work to and receive work from his unit. He shall discuss changes and clarification of procedures with certain staff units, such as organization and methods, cost accounting, and personnel. He shall consult supervisors of units which provide or receive special work assignments.

The organizational structure, however, establishes patterns other than those of the relationships of positions. These are the patterns of responsibility, authority, and expectations.

The supervisor is responsible for certain activities or results; he is presumably invested with the authority to achieve these. His set of authority and responsibility is interwoven with other sets to the end that all goals and functions of the organization are parceled out in small, manageable lots. This, of course, establishes a series of expectations: a single supervisor can perform his particular set of duties only upon the assumption that preceding or contiguous sets of duties have been, or are being, carried out. At the same time, he is aware of the expectations of others that he will fulfill his functional role.

The structure of an organization establishes relationships between specified positions and specific expectations for these positions. The fact that these relationships and expectations are established is one thing; whether or not they are met is another.

PRESCRIPTIONS AND PROSCRIPTIONS

But let us return to the organizational influences which act to restrict the supervisor's exercise of leadership. These are the prescriptions and proscriptions generally in effect in all organizations, and those peculiar to a single organization. In brief these are the *thous shalt's* and the *thou shalt not's.*

Organizations not only prescribe certain duties for individual supervisory positions, they also prescribe specific methods and means of carrying out these duties and maintaining management-employee relations. These include rules, regulations, policy, and. tradition. It does no good for the supervisor to say, *This seems to be the best way to handle such-and such,* if the organization has established a routine for dealing with problems. For good or bad, there are rules that state that firings shall be executed in such a manner, accompanied by a certain notification; that training shall be conducted, and in this manner. Proscriptions are merely negative prescriptions: you may not discriminate against any employee because of politics or race; you shall not suspend any employee without following certain procedures and obtaining certain approvals.

Most of these prohibitions and rules apply to the area of interpersonal relations, precisely the area which is now arousing most interest on the part of administrators and managers. We have become concerned about the contrast between formally prescribed relationships and interpersonal relationships, and this brings us to the often discussed informal organization.

FORMAL AND INFORMAL ORGANIZATIONS

As we well know, the functions and activities of any organization are broken down into individual units of work called positions. Administrators must establish a pattern which will link these positions to each other and relate them to a system of authority and responsibility. Man-to-man are spelled out as plainly as possible for all to understand. Managers, then, build an official structure which we call the formal organization.

In these same organizations employees react individually and in groups to institutionally determined roles. John, a worker, rides in the same car pool as Joe, a foreman. An unplanned communication develops. Harry, a machinist, knows more about highspeed machining than his foreman or anyone else in his shop. An unofficial tool boss comes into being. Mary, who fought with Jane is promoted over her. Jane now ignores Mary's directions. A planned relationship fails to develop. The employees have built a structure which we call the informal organization.

Formal organization is a system of management-prescribed relations between positions in an organization.

Informal organization is a network of unofficial relations between people in an organization.

These definitions might lead us to the absurd conclusion that positions carry out formal activities and that employees spend their time in unofficial activities. We must recognize that organizational activities are in all cases carried out by people. The formal structure provides a needed framework within which interpersonal relations occur. What we call informal organization is the complex of normal, natural relations among employees. These personal relationships may be negative or positive. That is, they may impede or aid the achievement of organizational, goals. For example, friendship between two supervisors greatly increases the probability of good cooperation and coordination between their sections. On the other hand, *buck passing* nullifies the formal structure by failure to meet a prescribed and expected responsibility.

It is improbable that an ideal organization exists where all activities are acarried out in strict conformity to a formally prescribed pattern of functional roles. Informal organization arises because of the incompleteness and ambiguities in the network of formally prescribed relationships, or in response to the needs or inadequacies of supervisors or managers who hold prescribed functional roles in an organization. Many of these relationships are not prescribed by the organizational pattern; many cannot be prescribed; many should not be prescribed.

Management faces the problem of keeping the informal organization in harmony with the mission of the agency. One way to do this is to make sure that all employees have a clear understanding of and are sympathetic with that mission. The issuance of organizational charts, procedural manuals, and functional descriptions of the work to be done by divisions and sections helps communicate management's plans and goals. Issuances alone, of course, cannot do the whole job. They should be accompanied by oral discussion and explanation. Management must ensure that there is mutual understanding and acceptance of charts and procedures. More important is that management acquaint itself with the attitudes, activities, and peculiar brands of logic which govern the informal organization. Only through this type of knowledge can they and supervisors keep informal goals consistent with the agency mission.

SUPERVISION, STATUS, AND FUNCTIONAL ROLE

A well-established supervisor is respected by the employees who work with him. They defer to his wishes. It is clear that a superior-subordinate relationship has been established. That is, status of the supervisor has been established in relation to other employees of the same work group. This same supervisor gains the respect of employees when he behaves in a certain manner. He will be expected generally, to follow the customs of the group in such matters as dress, recreation, and manner of speaking. The group has a set of expectations as to his behavior. His position is a functional role which carries with it a collection of rights and obligations.

The position of supervisor usually has a status distinct from the individual who occupies it: it is much like a position description which exists whether or not there is an incumbent. The status of a supervisory position is valued higher than that of an employee position both because of the functional role of leadership which is assigned to it and because of the status symbols of titles, rights, and privileges which go with it.

Social ranking, or status, is not simple because it involves both the position and the man. An individual may be ranked higher than others because of his education, social background, perceived leadership ability, or conformity to group customs and ideals. If such a man is ranked higher by the members of a work group than their supervisor, the supervisor's effectiveness may be seriously undermined.

If the organization does not build and reinforce a supervisor's status, his position can be undermined in a different way. This will happen when managers go around rather than through the supervisor or designate him as a straw boss, acting boss, or otherwise not a real boss.

Let us clarify this last point. A role, and corresponding status, establishes a set of expectations. Employees expect their supervisor to do certain things and to act in certain ways. They are prepared to respond to that expected behavior. When the supervisor's behavior does not conform to their expectations, they are surprised, confused, and ill-at-ease. It becomes necessary for them to resolve their confusion, if they can. They might do this by turning to one of their own members for leadership. If the confusion continues, or their attempted solutions are not satisfactory, they will probably become a poorly motivated, non-cohesive group which cannot function very well.

COMMUNICATION AND THE SUPERVISOR

In a recent survey railroad workers reported that they rarely look to their supervisors for information about the company. This is startling, at least to us, because we ordinarily think of the supervisor as the link between management and worker. We expect the supervisor to be the prime source of information about the company. Actually, the railroad workers listed the supervisor next to last in the order of their sources of information. Most suprising of all, the supervisors, themselves, stated that rumor and unofficial contacts were their principal sources of information. Here we see one of the reasons why supervisors may not be as effective as management desires.

The supervisor is not only being bypassed by his work group, he is being ignored, and his position weakened, by the very organization which is holding him responsible for the activities of his workers. If he is management's representative to the employee, then management has an obligation to keep him informed of its activities. This is necessary if he is to carry out his functions efficiently and maintain his leadership in the work group. The supervisor is expected to be a source of information; when he is not, his status is not clear, and employees are dissatisfied because he has not lived up to expectations.

By providing information to the supervisor to pass along to employees, we can strengthen his position as leader of the group, and increase satisfaction and cohesion within the group. Because he has more information than the other members, receives information sooner, and passes it along at the proper times, members turn to him as a source and also provide him with information in the hope of receiving some in return. From this we can see an increase in group cohesiveness because:

o   Employees are bound closer to their supervisor because he is *in the know*

o   there is less need to go outside the group for answers

o   employees will more quickly turn to the supervisor for enlightenment.

The fact that he has the answers will also enhance the supervisor's standing in the eyes of his men. This increased sta,tus will serve to bolster his authority and control of the group and will probably result in improved morale and productivity.

The foregoing, of course, does not mean that all management information should be given out. There are obviously certain policy determinations and discussions which need not or cannot be transmitted to all supervisors. However, the supervisor must be kept as fully informed as possible so that he can answer questions when asked and can allay needless fears and anxieties. Further, the supervisor has the responsibility of encouraging employee questions and submissions of information. He must be able to present information to employees so that it is clearly understood and accepted. His attitude and manner should make it clear that he believes in what he is saying, that the information is necessary or desirable to the group, and that he is prepared to act on the basis of the information.

SUPERVISION AND JOB PERFORMANCE

The productivity of work groups is a product; employees' efforts are multiplied by the supervision they receive. Many investigators have analyzed this relationship and have discovered elements of supervision which differentiate high and low production groups. These researchers have identified certain types of supervisory practices which they classify as *employee-centered* and other types which they classify as *production centered.*

The difference between these two kinds of supervision lies not in specific practices but in the approach or orientation to supervision. The employee-centered supervisor directs most of his efforts toward increasing employee motivation. He is concerned more with realizing the potential energy of persons than with administrative and technological methods of increasing efficiency and productivity. He is the man who finds ways of causing employees to want to work harder with the same tools. These supervisors emphasize the personal relations between their employees and themselves.

Now, obviously, these pictures are overdrawn. No one supervisor has all the virtues of the ideal type of employee-centered supervisor. And, fortunately, no one supervisor has all the bad traits found in many production-centered supervisors. We should remember that the various practices that researchers have found which distinguish these two kinds of supervision represent the many practices and methods of supervisors of all gradations between these extremes. We should be careful, too, of the implications of the labels attached to the two types. For instance, being production-centered is not necessarily bad, since the principal responsibility of any supervisor is maintaining the production level that is expected of his work group. Being employee-centered may not necessarily be good, if the only result is a happy, chuckling crew of loafers. To return to the researchers's findings, employee-centered supervisors:

- o   Recommend promotions, transfers, pay increases

- o   Inform men about what is happening in the company

- o   Keep men posted on how well they are doing

- o   Hear complaints and grievances sympathetically

- o   Speak up for subordinates

Production-centered supervisors, on the other hand, don't do those things. They check on employees more frequently, give more detailed and frequent instructions, don't give reasons for changes, and are more punitive when mistakes are made. Employee-centered supervisors were reported to contribute to high morale and high production, whereas production-centered supervision was associated with lower morale and less production.

More recent findings, however, show that the relationship between supervision and productivity is not this simple. Investigators now report that high production is more frequently associated with supervisory practices which combine employee-centered behavior with concern for production. (This concern is not the same, however, as anxiety about production, which is the hallmark of our production-centered supervisor.) Let us examine these apparently contradictory findings and the premises from which they are derived.

SUPERVISION AND MORALE

Why do supervisory activities cause high or low production? As the name implies, the activities of the employee-centered supervisor tend to relate him more closely and satisfactorily to his workers. The production-centered supervisor's practices tend to separate him from his group and to foster antagonism. An analysis of this difference may answer our question.

Earlier, we pointed out that the supervisor is a type of leader and that leadership is intimately related to the group in which it occurs. We discover, now, that an employee-centered supervisor's primary activities are concerned with both his leadership and his group membership. Such a supervisor is a member of a group and occupies a leadership role in that group.

These facts are sometimes obscured when we speak of the supervisor as management's representative, or as the organizational link between management and the employee, or as the end of the chain of command. If we really want to understand what it is we expect of the supervisor, we must remember that he is the designated leader of a group of employees to whom he is bound by interaction and interdependence.

Most of his actions are aimed, consciously or unconsciously, at strengthening membership ties in the group. This includes both making members more conscious that he is a member of their grout) and causing members to identify themselves more closely with the group. These ends are accomplished by:

making the group more attractive to the worker: they
    find satisfaction of their needs for recognition,
    friendship, enjoyable work, etc.;

maintaining open communication: employees can express
    their views and obtain information about the organization.

giving assistance: members can seek advice on
    personal problems as well as their work; and
acting as a buffer between the group and management:
    he speaks up for his men and explains the reasons
    for management's decisions.

Such actions both strengthen group cohesiveness and solidarity and affirm the supervisor's leadership position in the group.

DEFINING MORALE

This brings us back to a point mentioned earlier. We had said that employee-centered supervisors contribute to high morale as well as to high production. But how can we explain units which have low morale and high productivity, or vice versa? Usually production and morale are considered separately, partly because they are measured against different criteria and partly because, in some instances, they seem to be independent of each other.

Some of this difficulty may stem from confusion over definitions of morale. Morale has been defined as, or measured by, absences from work, satisfaction with job or company, dissension among members of work groups, productivity, apathy or lack of interest, readiness to help others, and a general aura of happiness as rated by observers. Some of these criteria of morale are not subject to the influence of the supervisor, and some of them are not clearly related to productivity. Definitions like these invite findings of low morale coupled with high production.

Both productivity and morale can be influenced by environmental factors not under the control of group members or supervisors. Such things as plant layout, organizational structure and goals, lighting, ventilation, communications, and management planning may have an adverse or desirable effect.

We might resolve the dilemma by defining morale on the basis of our understanding of the supervisor as leader of a group; morale is the degree of satisfaction of group members with their leadership. In this light, the supervisor's employee-centered activities bear a clear relation to morale. His efforts to increase employee identification with the group and to strengthen his leadership lead to greater satisfaction with that leadership. By increasing group cohesiveness and by demonstrating that his influence and power can aid the group, he is able to enhance his leadership status and afford satisfaction to the group.

SUPERVISION, PRODUCTION, AND MORALE

There are factors within the organization itself which determine whether increased production is possible:

Are production goals expressed in terms understandable to employees and are they realistic?

Do supervisors responsible for production respect the agency mission and production goals?

If employees do not know how to do the job well, does management provide a trainer--often the supervisor--who can teach efficient work methods?

There are other factors within the work group which determine whether increased production will be attained:

Is leadership present which can bring about the desired level of production?

Are production goals accepted by employees as reasonable and attainable?

If group effort is involved, are members able to coordinate their efforts?

Research findings confirm the view that an employee-centered supervisor can achieve higher morale than a production-centered supervisor. Managers may well ask what is the relationship between this and production?

Supervision is production-oriented to the extent that it focuses attention on achieving organizational goals, and plans and devises methods for attaining them; it is employee-centered to the extent that it focuses attention on employee attitudes toward those goals, and plans and works toward maintenance of employee satisfaction.

High productivity and low morale result when a supervisor plans and organizes work efficiently but cannot achieve high membership satisfaction. Low production and high morale result when a supervisor, though keeping members satisfied with his leadership, either has not gained acceptance of organizational goals or does not have the technical competence to achieve them.

The relationship between supervision, morale, and productivity is an interdependent one, with the supervisor playing an integrating role due to his ability to influence productivity and morale independently of each other.

A supervisor who can plan his work well has good technical knowledge, and who can install better production methods can raise production without necessarily increasing group satisfaction. On the other hand, a supervisor who can motivate his employees and keep them satisfied with his leadership can gain high production in spite of technical difficulties and environmental obstacles.

CLIMATE AND SUPERVISION

Climate, the intangible environment of an organization made up of attitudes, beliefs, and traditions, plays a large part in morale, productivity, and supervision. Usually when we speak of climate and its relationship to morale and productivity, we talk about the merits of *democratic* versus *authoritarian* climate. Employees seem to produce more and have higher morale in a democratic climate, whereas in an authoritarian climate, the reverse seems to be true or so the researchers tell us. We would do well to determine what these terms mean to supervision.

Perhaps most of our difficulty in understanding and applying these concepts comes from our emotional reactions to the words themselves. For example, authoritarian climate is usually painted as the very blackest kind of dictatorship. This not surprising, because we are usually expected to believe that it is invariably bad. Conversely, democratic climate is drawn to make the driven snow look impure by comparison.

Now these descriptions are most probably true when we talk about our political processes, or town meetings, or freedom of speech. However the same labels have been used by social scientists in other contexts and have also been applied to government and business organizations, without, it seems, any recognition that the meanings and their social values may have changed somewhat .

For example, these labels were used in experiments conducted in an informal class room setting using 11 year old boys as subjects. The descriptive labels applied to the climate of the setting as well as the type of leadership practiced. When these labels were transferred to a management setting it seems that many presumed that they principally meant the king of leadership rather than climate. We can see that there is a great difference between the experimental and management settings and that leadership practices for one might be inappropriate for the other.

It is doubtful that formal work organizations can be anything but authoritarian, in that goals are set by management and a hierarchy exists through which decisions and orders from the top are transmitted downward. Organizations are authoritarian by structure and need: direction and control are placed in the hands of a few in order to gain fast and efficient decision making. Now this does not mean to describe a dictatorship. It is merely the recognition of the fact that direction of organizational affairs comes from above. It should be noted that leadership in some natural groups is, in this sense, authoritarian.

Granting that formal organizations have this kind of authoritarian leadership, can there be a democratic climate? Certainly there can be, but we would want to define and delimit this term. A more realistic meaning of democratic climate in organizations is, the use of permissive and participatory methods in management-employee relations. That is, a mutual exchange of information and explanation with the granting of individual freedom within certain restricted and defined limits. However, it is not our purpose to debate the merits of authoritarianism versus democracy. We recognize that within the small work group there is a need for freedom from constraint and an increase in participation in order to achieve organizational goals within the framework of the organizational environment.

Another aspect of climate is best expressed by this familiar, and true saying: actions speak louder than words. Of particular concern to us is this effect of management climate on the behavior of supervisors, particularly in employee-centered activities.

There have been reports of disappointment with efforts to make supervisors more employee-centered. Managers state that, since research has shown ways of improving human relations, supervisors should begin to practice these methods. Usually a training course in human relations is established, and supervisors are given this training. Managers then sit back and wait for the expected improvements, only to find that there are none.

If we wish to produce changes in the supervisor's behavior,the climate must be made appropriate and rewarding to the changed behavior. This means that top-level attitudes and behavior cannot deny or contradict the change we are attempting to effect. Basic changes in organizational behavior cannot be made with any permanence, unless we provide an environment that is receptive to the changes and rewards those persons who do change.

IMPROVING SUPERVISION

Anyone who has read this far might expect to find *A Dozen Rules for Dealing With Employees* or *29 Steps to Supervisory Success*. We will not provide such a list.

Simple rules suffer from their simplicity. They ignore the complexities of human behavior. Reliance upon rules may cause supervisors to concentrate on superficial aspects of their relations with employees. It may preclude genuine understanding.

The supervisor who relies on a list of rules tends to think of people in mechanistic terms. In a certain situation, he uses *Rule No. 3.* Employees are not treated as thinking and feeling persons, but rather as figures in a formula: Rule 3 applied to employee X = Production.

Employees usually recognize mechanical manipulation and become dissatisfied and resentful. They lose faith in, and respect for, their supervisor, and this may be reflected in lower morale and productivity.

We do not mean that supervisors must become social science experts if they wish to improve. Reports of current research indicate that there are two major parts of their job which can be strengthened through self-improvement: (1) Work planning, including technical skills. (2) Motivation of employees.

The most effective supervisors combine excellence in the administrative and technical aspects of their work with friendly and considerate personal relations with their employees.

CRITICAL PERSONAL RELATIONS

Later in this chaper we shall talk about administrative aspects of supervision, but first let us comment on *friendly and considerate personal relations*. We have discussed this subject throughout the preceding chapters, but we want to review some of the critical supervisory influences on personal relations.

Closeness of Supervision

The closeness of supervision has an important effect on productivity and morale. Mann and Dent found that supervisors of low-producing units supervise very closely, while high-producing supervisors exercise only general supervision. It was found that the low-producing supervisors:

- o   check on employees more frequently

- o   give more detailed and frequent instructions

- o   limit employee's freedom to do job in own way.

Workers who felt less closely supervised reported that they were better satisfied with their jobs and the company. We should note that the manner or attitude of the supervisor has an important bearing on whether employees perceive supervision as being close or general.

These findings are another way of saying that supervision does not mean standing over the employee and telling him what to do and when and how to do it. The more effective supervisor tells his employees what is required, giving general instructions.

COMMUNICATION

Supervisors of high-production units consider communication as one of the most important aspects of their job. Effective communication is used by these supervisors to achieve better interpersonal relations and improved employee motivation. Low-production supervisors do not rate communication as highly important.

High-producing supervisors find that an important aid to more effective communication is listening. They are ready to listen to both personal problems or interests and questions about the work. This does not mean that they are *nosey* or meddle in their employees' personal lives, but rather that they show a willingness to listen, and do listen, if their employees wish to discuss problems.

These supervisors inform employees about forthcoming changes in work; they discuss agency policy with employees; and they make sure that each employee knows how well he is doing. What these supervisors do is use two-way communication effectively. Unless the supervisor freely imparts information, he will not receive information in return.

Attitudes and perception are frequently affected by communication or the lack of it. Research surveys reveal that many supervisors are not aware of their employees' attitudes, nor do they know what personal reactions their supervision arouses. Through frank discussions with employees, they have been surprised to discover employee beliefs about which they were ignorant. Discussion sometimes reveals that the supervisor and his employees have totally different impressions about the same event. The supervisor should be constantly on the alert for misconceptions about his words and deeds. He must remember that, although his actions are perfectly clear to himself, they may be, and frequently are, viewed differently by employees.

Failure to communicate information results in misconceptions and false assumptions. What you say and how you say it will strongly affect your employees' attitudes and perceptions. By giving them available information you can prevent misconceptions; by discussion, you may be able to change attitudes; by questioning; you can discover what the perceptions and assumptions really are. And it need hardly be added that actions should conform very closely to words.

If we were to attempt to reduce the above discussion on communication to rules, we would have a long list which would be based on one cardinal principle: Don't make assumptions!

   o   Don't assume that your employees know; tell them.

   o   Don't assume that you know how they feel; find out.

   o   Don't assume that they understand; clarify.

20 SUPERVISORY HINTS

1. Avoid inconsistency.
2. Always give employees a chance to explain their actions before taking disciplinary action. Don't allow too much time for a "cooling off" period before disciplining an employee.
3. Be specific in your criticisms.
4. Delegate responsibility wisely.
5. Do not argue or lose your temper, and avoid being impatient.
6. Promote mutual respect and be fair, impartial and open-minded.
7. Keep in mind that asking for employees' advice and input can be helpful in decision making.
8. If you make promises, keep them.
9. Always keep the feelings, abilities, dignity and motives of your staff in mind.
10. Remain loyal to your employees' interests.
11. Never criticize employees in front of others, or treat employees like children.
12. Admit mistakes. Don't place blame on your employees, or make excuses.
13. Be reasonable in your expectations, give complete instructions, and establish well-planned goals.
14. Be knowledgeable about office details and procedures, but avoid becoming bogged down in details.
15. Avoid supervising too closely or too loosely. Employees should also view you as an approachable supervisor.
16. Remember that employees' personal problems may affect job performance, but become involved only when appropriate.
17. Work to develop workers, and to instill a feeling of cooperation while working toward mutual goals.
18. Do not overpraise or underpraise, be properly appreciative.
19. Never ask an employee to discipline someone for you.
20. A complaint, even if unjustified, should be taken seriously.

BASIC FUNDAMENTALS OF
PAVING EQUIPMENT AND OPERATIONS

CONTENTS

Page

I. PAVING CONSTRUCTION   1

II. MAINTENANCE OF BITUMINOUS PAVEMENT   19

III. MAINTENANCE OF EQUIPMENT   22

IV. PAVING SAFETY   23

V. CONCRETE TRANSIT MIXERS   24

VI. OPERATOR'S CARE AND MAINTENANCE   28

VII. TRANSIT MIXER SAFETY   28

BASIC FUNDAMENTALS OF

PAVING EQUIPMENT AND OPERATIONS

This chapter provides information and guidance for the equipment operator engaged in, or responsible for, bituminous and expedient surfacing operations involving roads and airfields. It includes information on construction materials, mix design, equipment, production, placement, repair and maintenance of bituminous and expedient (emergency make shift construction using the natural resources available) surfaces.

Information on starting, operating, and maintaining concrete transit trucks is given in this chapter. Also included is information on the principles of operating asphalt pavers, asphalt distributors, asphalt traveling plants, asphalt kettles, and self-propelled soil stabilization mixers.

Safety precautions must be rigidly observed in paving operations, particularly in the use of flammables. Safety precautions will be noted at pertinent points, where applicable, throughout the chapter.

I. PAVING CONSTRUCTION

Modern paving is broadly divided into RIGID paving and FLEXIBLE paving. Both types consist of AGGREGATE (sand, gravel, crushed stone, and the like), bound together by a hardening or setting agent called a BINDER. The chief difference between the two types of paving, from the standpoint of ingredients used, lies in the character of the binder.

The binder for most rigid paving is PORTLAND CEMENT, and, for this reason, rigid paving is often referred to as CONCRETE paving. In flexible paving, the binder consists of BITUMINOUS material.

Asphalt paving mixes may be produced from a wide range of aggregate combinations, each having its own characteristics and suited to specific design and construction uses. Aside from the asphalt content, the principal characteristics of the mix are determined, in the main,

by the relative amounts of aggregates. The aggregate composition may vary from a coarse-textured mix having a predominance of coarse aggregate to a fine-textured mix having a predominance of fine aggregate.

The selection of a particular bituminous material depends upon the type of pavement, temperature extreme, rainfall, type and volume of traffic, and type and availability of equipment. In general, hard penetration grades of asphalt cement are used in warm climates and softer penetration grades in cold climates. Heavier grades of asphalt cutbacks and tars are generally used in warm regions. Asphalt cements are generally more suitable for high traffic volumes than cutbacks. Asphalts and tars will not necessarily bond to each other; thus, bonding becomes a consideration in bitumen selection.

Looking at figure 1 you can see that many types of products, including asphalt materials, are produced by the refining of petroleum. Such asphalt is produced in a variety of types and grades ranging from hard brittle solids to almost water thin liquids. The semisolid form, known as asphalt cement, is the basic material.

Liquid asphaltic products are generally prepared by cutting back or blending asphalt cements with petroleum distillates or by emulsifying them with water. Types of liquid asphaltic products as shown in figure 2.

Table 1 indicates various uses of asphalt for different types of construction.

In a work area, expedient materials and methods may be used when men, materials, equipment, or time are not available for more permanent surfacing construction. With the choice of materials or methods, the determining factors in selecting the type of expedient will be the time allotted for construction, the required permanency, the type of terrain, and the anticipated type of traffic. As an expedient, any material or method that will provide a temporary road or airfield may be used. Expedient pavements and surfaces may be used provided the criteria for

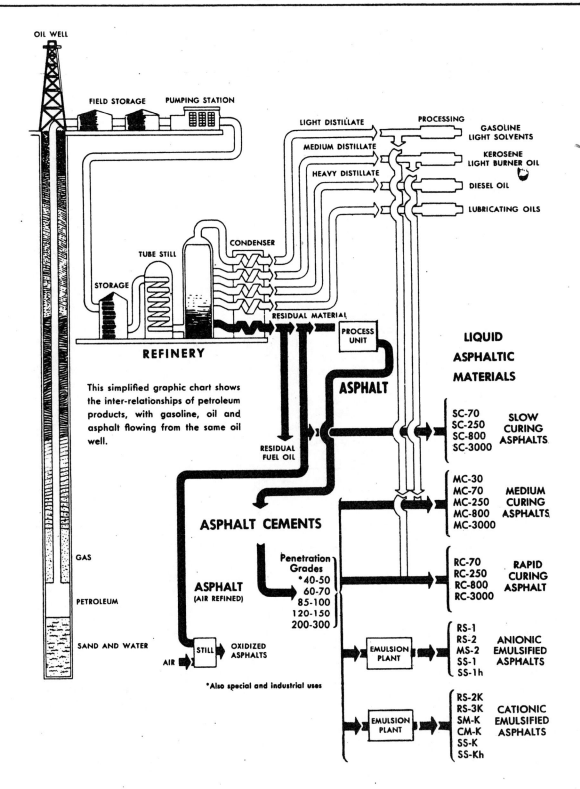

Figure 1. — Petroleum asphalt flow chart.

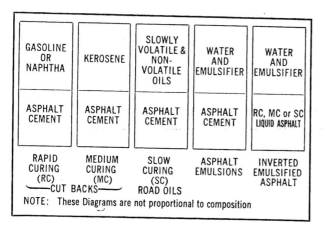

GASOLINE OR NAPHTHA	KEROSENE	SLOWLY VOLATILE & NON-VOLATILE OILS	WATER AND EMULSIFIER	WATER AND EMULSIFIER
ASPHALT CEMENT	ASPHALT CEMENT	ASPHALT CEMENT	ASPHALT CEMENT	RC, MC or SC LIQUID ASPHALT
RAPID CURING (RC)	MEDIUM CURING (MC)	SLOW CURING (SC)	ASPHALT EMULSIONS	INVERTED EMULSIFIED ASPHALT

———CUT BACKS——— ROAD OILS

NOTE: These Diagrams are not proportional to composition

Figure 2.—Liquid asphaltic products.

establishing suitable bases have been met. Sound construction principles and imagination will lead to many improved expedient methods.

ROAD-MIX PAVEMENTS

Road-mix pavements consist of mineral aggregate and mineral filler uniformly mixed in place with a bituminous material and compacted on a prepared base course or subgrade. A single layer, about 1-1/2 inches to 3 inches thick, is generally used. This type of pavement is likely to become defective unless it has a sound, well-drained subgrade and is well mixed, uniformly spread, and properly compacted. Road-mix pavements may be used as a wearing surface on temporary roads and airfields, and as a bituminous base or binder course in construction of more permanent-type roads and airfields. Road mix is an economical method of surfacing small areas when aggregate can be used from the existing base, or when satisfactory aggregate is nearby.

For road-mix pavements, the grade and type of bituminous material depend upon the aggregate and equipment available, as well as weather conditions and time required to complete the project. Good weather is important to the success of a road-mix project. Where possible, road mixing operations should be scheduled when weather conditions are likely to be hot and dry during, and for sometime after, the project. Recommended types of bituminous materials suitable for road mix are asphalt cutbacks, asphalt emulsions, and road tars. A medium-curing cutback is generally used in a moderate climate; and a rapid-curing cutback may be satisfactory for cold climates. Viscosity required is determined by the temperature, aggregate graduation, and method of mixing. The highest viscosity that will completely and uniformly coat the particles of aggregate should be used. In general, open-graded aggregate requires a high viscosity; a gradation containing mineral filler requires a less viscous grade.

Aggregate used in road mix may be scarified from the existing subgrade or hauled in from a nearby source. A wide range of coarse and fine aggregate and mineral filler may be used. The ideal aggregate for road-mix pavement is a well-graded (dense or open) sandy gravel or clean sand. Maximum size of the aggregate, in general, is limited to two-thirds of the compacted thickness of the layer. Loose thickness is approximately 1-1/4 times desired compacted thickness.

Surface moisture is defined as "the film of water around each particle of stone or sand." The amount is determined by heating a weighted sample of aggregate at 212°F in an open pan and stirring with a rod until the surface water disappears (3 to 10 minutes). The difference between the original and final weights is considered to be moisture loss during drying. The loss in weight, expressed as a percent of the final or dry weight, is the moisture content allowed before the aggregate is mixed with asphalt cutbacks or road tars. If the aggregate is too wet, it should be worked with mechanical mixers, graders, or improvised plows to allow the excess moisture to evaporate. For cutbacks and tars, moisture content of coarse-graded aggregate should not exceed 3 percent, and of fine-graded aggregate, 2 percent. For emulsions, moisture content of coarse-graded aggregate should not exceed 5 percent, and of fine-graded aggregate, 3 percent.

Quality of the road-mix pavement depends largely upon the control of the mix. The percentage of bitumen will vary in relation to the absorptive quality of the aggregate, rate of evaporation of the volatile substances, and other factors. Although an exact formula is difficult to follow, proportioning must be controlled within very narrow limits to assure the stability and life of the mix. With dense-graded aggregates especially, too much bitumen should not be used. All particles of the completed mix should be coated and uniform in color. If the mix is too lean, the aggregate in the windrow will stand almost vertically and have a dull

3

Table 1. — Recommended Uses of Various Asphalt Grades

Type of Construction	40-50	60-70	85-100	120-150	200-300	RC 70	RC 250	RC 800	RC 3000	MC 30	MC 70	MC 250	MC 800	MC 3000	SC 70	SC 250	SC 800	SC 3000	RS-1	RS-2	MS-2	SS-1	SS-1h	RS-2K	RS-3K	SM-K	CM-K	SS-K	SS-Kh
ASPHALT CONCRETE AND PLANT MIX, HOT LAID																													
Highways		x	x	x										x				x											
Airports		x	x																										
Parking Areas		x	x																										
Driveways		x	x																										
Curbs		x	x¹																										
Industrial Floors	x																												
Blocks	x																												
PLANT MIX, COLD LAID																													
Graded Aggregate													x				x					x						x	x
ROAD MIX																													
Open-graded Aggregate						x	x						x	x					x								x		
Dense-graded Aggregate						x	x					x	x			x	x		x	x						x		x	
Clean Sand						x	x					x	x									x						x	x
Sandy Soil						x	x	x				x	x			x	x		x								x	x	x
PENETRATION MACADAM																													
Large Voids		x					x	x											x								x		
Small Voids			x			x													x					x					
SURFACE TREATMENTS																													
Single, Multiple and Aggregate Seal						x	x					x	x	x		x	x	x	x	x		x		x	x			x	
Sand Seal						x	x					x	x			x	x		x			x	x	x				x	x
Slurry Seal																			x	x								x	x
Fog Seal																			x²	x²								x²	x²
Prime Coat, open surfaces						x					x																		
Prime Coat, tight surfaces						x				x	x				x														
Tack Coat						x													x			x²	x²	x				x²	x²
Dust Laying										x	x				x				x²									x²	
PATCHING MIX																													
Immediate Use												x					x												
Stock Pile												x	x			x	x									x	x		
HYDRAULIC STRUCTURES																													
Membrane Linings, Canals & Reservoirs	x³																												
Hot Laid, Graded Aggregate Mix for Groins, Dam Facings, Canal & Reservoir Linings	x	x																											
CRACK FILLING						x													x			x⁴	x⁴	x				x⁴	x⁴
MEMBRANE ENVELOPE	x	x																											
EXPANSION JOINTS	Blown asphalts, mineral-filled asphalt cements, and preformed joint compositions																												
UNDERSEALING PCC	Blown asphalts																												
ROOFING	Blown asphalts																												
MISCELLANEOUS	Specially prepared asphalts for pipe coatings, battery boxes, automobile undersealing, electrical wire coating, insulation, tires, paints, asphalt tile, wall board, paper sizing, waterproofing, floor mats, ice cream sacks, adhesives, phonograph records, tree grafting compounds, grouting mixtures, etc.																												

In northern areas where rate of curing is slower, a shift from MC to RC or from SC to MC may be desirable. For very warm climates, a shift to next heavier grade may be warranted.

1 In combination with powdered asphalt.
2 Diluted with water.
3 Also 50-60 penetration blown asphalt and prefabricated panels.
4 Slurry mix.

look while if too rich, it will ooze or slip out of shape. If the mix is correctly proportioned, a handful squeezed into a ball will retain its shape when the hand is opened.

Road-mix pavements should be constructed only on a dry base when the weather is not rainy. Atmospheric temperature should be above 50°F. Mixing should take place at the temperature of the aggregate, but not below 50°F or above the recommended temperature of the liquid asphalt being used. The construction procedure depends upon whether the base is a newly constructed base, a scarified existing base, or an existing pavement.

If a newly constructed base is used, apply the following procedure:

1. Inspect and condition the base.
2. Prime the base and allow the prime to cure.

3. Haul in and windrow the aggregate at the side of the primed base (allow the aggregate to dry or aerate with blade if wet.)

4. Spread the aggregate on the cured prime base 1/2 road bed width.

5. Spray the bitumen on the aggregate in increments of about one-third the total amount required.

6. Mix the bitumen with the aggregate, blade back and forth until a uniform mix is obtained.

7. Repeat as directed in (5) and (6) until thoroughly mixed.

8. Spread the mix to the specified thickness.

9. Compact the surface.

10. Apply a seal coat if necessary.

For a scarified base, the aggregate is scarified if it is not available from other sources. The construction procedure is as follows:

1. Loosen the aggregate from the base.

2. Dry and break up all lumps of material.

3. Blade into parallel windrows of uniform size and one side and/or in the center.

4. Sweep the base, if needed.

5. Prime the base and allow time to cure.

6. Continue as directed in (4) through (10) in the above procedures for a newly constructed base.

If an existing pavement is to be used as a base, the construction procedure is:

1. Sweep the base.

2. Apply a tack coat and allow it to cure.

3. Bring in the aggregate and deposit in windrows at the side of the cured, tacked base.

4. Aerate the aggregate.

5. Spread the aggregate on 1/2 the tacked base.

6. Spray bitumen on the aggregate in increments of about 1/3 the total amount required.

7. Mix the bitumen with the aggregate, by blade.

8. Spread the mix to specified uncompacted thickness.

9. Compact the surface.

10. Apply a seal coat if necessary.

When mixing in place (road mix), here are some helpful hints:

1. Do not buck nature — stop operations when working under adverse weather conditions.

2. Keep the mixture or aggregate in a well packed windrow for better water shedding and control.

3. Provide drainage cuts through the windrow during heavy rains.

4. When a motor grader comes to the end of a section with a full blade, lift it rapidly, to avoid carrying materials into the next section.

5. The distributor spray must be cut sharply at sectional joints; carry-over to the next section will cause undesirable fat joints.

6. Plan the work to avoid inconvenience to traffic.

7. Apply the asphalt at the recommended spraying viscosity to ensure uniform application.

8. A shoe on the outer end of the grader blade or moldboard helps obtain a good edge during spreading operations.

9. Aggregate in shaded areas usually requires extra aeration.

ROAD MIXING METHODS

Three methods of road mixing that the Equipment Operator may use in expedient surfacing operations for roads and airfields are travel plant mixing, blade mixing, and soil asphalt stabilization mixing. These methods are discussed separately below.

Travel Plant Mixing

When a travel plant is used for mixing, the loose aggregate is dumped, mixed, and bladed into uniform windrows, and evened if necessary. The windrow should be sufficient to cover the section of the area to be paved with enough loose material to give the desired compacted depth and width. As the bucket loader tows the mixer and elevates the aggregate to the mixer hopper, the mixer meters the aggregate, sprays it with the correct amount of bitumen, mixes these two uniformly and redeposits the mix into another windrow behind the plant. The rate of travel and the mixing operation should be controlled so that all particles of the aggregate are coated and the mix is uniform. Accuracy in proportioning the mix is extremely important.

The travel plant method usually produces a more uniform mix of higher quality than blade mixing. Heavier types of asphalt cutback and tar may be used. This reduces the time required for curing. The asphalt finisher may be used concurrently with the travel plant. The hopper of the finisher is kept directly under the travel plant output chute. This arrangement reduces

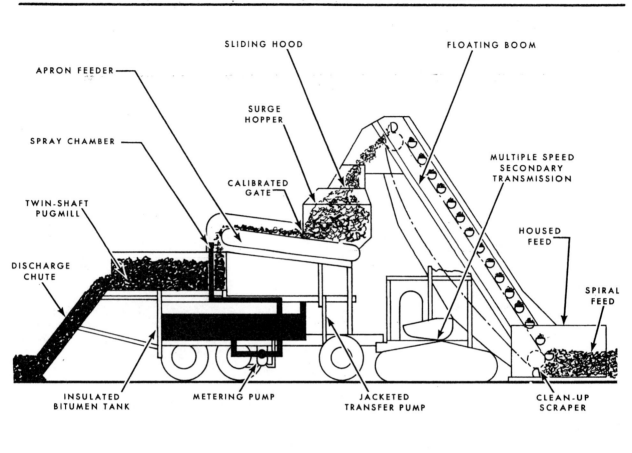

MIXER

CRAWLER MOUNTED
AGGREGATE ELEVATOR

Figure 3.—Schematic layout of a travel plant.

the maximum output of the plant, although it does provide for uniform thickness of the mat being laid.

Windrows must contain no more material than the finisher can place. The major advantage of this setup is that in-place aggregate may be used in an intermediate mix and placed with a finisher without the necessity of loading and transporting aggregate. The finisher must be used with the travel plant for construction of some airfields where surface tolerances are critical. Figure 3 shows a schematic view of a travel plant.

Blade Mixing

In blade mixing, the aggregate is dried and bladed into windrows. The windrows are then flattened and bitumen of the specific temperature is applied with a bituminous distributor in three equal applications. Each application is 1/3 the amount required.

Immediately following each application of the bituminous material, the treated aggregate should be mixed with springtooth or double-disk harrows, motor graders, rotary tillers, or a combination of this equipment, until all the particles of the aggregate are evenly coated. When motor graders are used, the windrow is moved from side to side by successive cuts with the blade.

Several graders can operate, one behind the other, to reduce the total time required for complete mixing. In hilly terrain, blading should be from the bottom to the top as the mix tends to migrate down. After all the aggregate has been mixed, the mix should be bladed into a single windrow at or near the center of the road, and turned not less than four complete turns from one side of the road to the other. Excess bitumen, deficiency of bitumen, or uneven mix should be corrected by the addition of aggregate or bituminous material, followed by remixing. Mixing should continue until it is complete and satisfactory; remember, mix will set up if mixed too long.

Suppose that materials, weather conditions, and equipment are well suited to mixed-in-place paving, but the road or airfield must carry traffic during construction. In such cases, the windrowing of aggregate and the mixing and spreading of bitumen may be done elsewhere, on any area of smooth ground which can be compacted for the purpose, or on any unused road or airfield surface. The road or airfield surface, base, or subbase to be paved is then primed or tack coated as required to complete construction and keep portions of the road or airfield open to traffic. As soon as the prime or tack coat cures the mix is picked up, trucked to the jobsite, dumped, and then bladed into windrows for spreading.

The bituminous mix should not be spread when the surface is damp, or when the mix itself contains an excess of moisture. The mixed material should be spread to the required width in thin, equal layers by a self-propelled motor grader or finisher. (If a finisher is used, additional support equipment is required, and the material must be split into two windrows for an 8- to 12-foot wide pavement.) When spreading the mix from a windrow, care should be taken to prevent cutting into the underlying subgrade or base course. If necessary to prevent such cutting, a layer of mix, approximately 1/2-inch thick, may be left at the bottom of the windrow.

The material being spread should be rolled once, and then leveled with a motor grader to remove irregularities. Remaining material should then be spread and rolled in thin layers, until the entire mix is evenly spread to the depth and width specified. During the spreading and compacting, the surface should be dragged or bladed, as necessary, to fill any ruts and to remove corrugations, waves, or other irregularities. Both pneumatic-tired and steel-wheeled rollers may be used for rolling on all surface treatment jobs; however, the pneumatic-tired roller is the preferred type. While the pneumatic-tired roller will give uniform pressure over the entire area the steel-wheeled roller will hit only the high spots. In any case, two self-propelled rollers should be used with each surface treatment job.

After all layers have been satisfactorily spread, the surface should be rolled with two-axle tandem rollers. Rolling should begin at the outside edge of the surface and proceed to the center, overlapping on successive trips at least one-half the width of the wheel of the roller. Alternate trips of the roller should be different lengths. The speed of the roller at all times should be controlled to avoid displacement of the mix. Light blading (or floating) of the surface with the motor grader during rolling may be required. Rolling should be continued until all roller marks are eliminated, and maximum density obtained. To prevent adhesion of the mix to the roller, the roller wheel should be kept moist with water; use only enough water to avoid picking up the material. The rollers should be in good condition, suitable for rolling asphalt, and should be operated by trained roller operators. At all places not accessible to the roller, the mix should be thoroughly tamped with hand tampers. If the surface course becomes rough, corrugated, uneven in texture, water-soaked, or traffic marked, unsatisfactory portions should be torn up, and reworked, relaid, or replaced. When forms are not used, and while the surface is being compacted and finished, the outside edges should be trimmed neatly in line.

If the road-mix pavement surface course is constructed from an open-graded aggregate, a surface treatment may be required to waterproof the surface. A surface treatment is unnecessary on a dense-graded, well-compacted, road-mix pavement.

Where possible, traffic should be kept off of freshly sprayed asphalt or mixed materials. If it is necessary to route traffic over the new work, speed must be restricted to 25 m.p.h. or less until rolling is completed and the asphalt mixture is firm enough to take high speed traffic.

Soil Asphalt Stabilization Mixing

Soil asphalt stabilization requires a mixture of pulverized soil and bituminous material. By the addition of bituminous material, many soils, which in their natural state would be too unstable for use as a base course, can be made to serve satisfactorily as a base course. The bituminous material serves primarily as a waterproofing agent rather than a binding agent; however, the bitumen does have some binding value.

Figure 4.—Multi-shaft, single-pass soil stabilizer.

If properly constructed, soil asphalt stabilization generally forms an excellent base. However, it is too friable to withstand the abrasive action of traffic, wears rapidly, and often develops uneven surfaces that eventually cause pot holes. Soil asphalt stabilization is recommended only as a base course, on which there is to be placed an approved type of wearing course or surface treatment.

Since most multiple-shaft, single-pass soil stabilization mixing machines such as that shown in figure 16-4 have a high-speed pulverizing rotor, preliminary pulverization is usually unnecessary. The only preparation required is to dig a trench about 18 inches wide and to the depth to be processed (1/4 inch minimum to 8 inches maximum) and across the full width of the roadway to be stabilized. Material removed from this trench should be spread out uniformly over the roadway so that this material will be mixed as the mixing box of the stabilizer unit travels forward.

Processing is done in lanes from 350 to 900 feet depending upon the rate of processing, with a width equal to that of the stabilizing machine. The stabilizing mixer is positioned in the first lane at the point where the cutting rotor is directly above the trench or starting point.

With the bituminous tank truck coupled to the front of the stabilizer, the suction hose connected to the delivery pump, and the mixer moving forward, the high speed cutting rotor cuts and pulverizes the road material to be stabilized. The blending rotor picks up the loose material and trims the subgrade. Turning in the opposite direction of the cutting rotor, the blending rotor provides a shuttle motion that ensures a thorough mixing of the material. The material from the blending rotor is then carried up and over the rotor and tossed into the twin pugmill. While the material is still in mid-air, it passes through an atomized spray of asphalt liquid. The strategic placement of the spray bars, together with controlled pressures, provides the most efficient dispersion of liquid for assuring accurate, uniform coating of all material particles.

All asphalt liquids used in material processing are accurately metered. After passing through the asphalt liquid spray, the thoroughly coated materials are agitated in a transverse, twin pugmill with overlapping blades. The opposed action of the blades provides intensified agitation and squeezing. This important operation renders a thorough job of final mixing and prepares the uniformly mixed mass of materials for subsequent spreading.

The adjustable tailgate provides flexibility for regulating the amount of materials held in the pugmill for thorough mixing and conforming to the processing depth. It strikes off materials to a uniform loose density the full width of the processing chamber. This material is then ready for immediate compaction where aeration is not required.

A small asphalt liquid tank on the machine permits continuous operation while the asphalt tank truck is being switched. The gallons of liquid asphalt required for a soil asphalt stabilization project will be determined by the project supervisor.

BITUMINOUS MATERIALS

Pavements constructed of bituminous materials and aggregates are referred to as "flexible pavements," because of their ability to permit slight deflections without detrimental effect. Flexibility is due to consolidation of the base course or effect of a load. Flexible pavements provide a resilient, waterproof, load-distributing medium which protects the base course from the detrimental effect of water and the abrasive action of traffic. Properly designed, high quality bituminous concrete is affected very little by temperature strains and fatigue stresses. Bituminous concrete pavements are subject to nominal maintenance due to wear, weathering, and deterioration from aging. Also, as load intensities increase, additional layers of bituminous pavement can be added to existing pavement to provide further reinforcement.

Bituminous pavements can be placed easily and quickly. For these reasons, bituminous materials have become of tremendous importance to both the military and civil engineer in the construction of roads and airfields. They can be used not only in pavements but also as soil stabilizers, thereby improving the strength and waterproofness of subgrades, subbases, and base courses.

Tack Coat

A tack coat is an application of asphalt to an existing paved surface to provide bond between the existing surface and the asphalt material to be placed on it. Two essential requirements of a tack coat are: (1) it must be very thin, and (2) it must uniformly cover the entire surface to be treated. A very thin tack coat does no harm to the pavement and it will properly bond the course.

Some of the bituminous materials used for tack coats are rapid-curing cutbacks, road tar cutbacks, rapid-setting emulsions (may be used in warm weather), and medium asphalt cements. Because rapid-curing cutbacks are highly flammable, safety precautions must be very carefully followed.

A tack coat should be applied only when the surface to be tacked is dry and the temperature has not been below 35°F for 12 hours immediately prior to application.

Before applying the tack coat to a surface that is sufficiently bonded, see that all loose material, dirt, clay, or other objectionable materials are removed from the surface to be treated. This operation may be accomplished with a power broom or blower, supplemented with hand brooms if necessary.

Immediately following the preparation of the surface, the bituminous material should be uniformly applied by means of a bituminous distributor (discussed later in this chapter) at the spraying temperature specified. The amount of bitumen application varies with the condition of the existing pavement being tack-coated, but in general 0.10 to 0.25 gal per sq yd is satisfactory. Following the application of bituminous material, the surface should be allowed to dry until it is in a proper condition of tackiness to receive the surface course, otherwise the volatile substances may act as a lubricant and prevent bonding with the wearing surface. Clean, dry sand should be spread on all areas that show an excess of bitumen to effectively blot up and cure the excess.

An existing surface that is to be covered by a bituminous wearing surface should be barricaded to prevent traffic from carrying dust or mud onto the surface, either before or after the tack coat is applied. Should it become necessary for traffic to use the surface, one lane may be tack coated and paved, using the other lane as a traffic bypass. The bypass lane should be primed and sanded before opening to traffic. It should be swept and reprimed after the adjacent lane is completed. This preserves the base and acts as a dust palliative (sheltering).

Prime Coat

Priming consists of the initial treatment on a granular base prior to surfacing with a bituminous material or pavement. The purpose of a prime coat is to penetrate the base (about 1/4" minimum penetration is desired), fill most of the voids, promote adhesion between the base and the bituminous applications placed on top of it, and waterproof the base.

The priming material may be either a low viscosity tar, a low viscosity asphalt, or a diluted asphalt emulsion. The quantities of priming materials to be applied will be determined by the condition of the soil base and climate. The use of rapid-curing asphalt cutbacks, in general 0.2 to 0.5 gal per square yard, in cold climates has proved to be satisfactory. However, the prime coat can be eliminated if the climate is very cold, as this is likely to slow the curing process.

The sequence of operations for the application of a prime coat is the same as described earlier for application of a tack coat. If the base absorbs all of the prime material within 1 to 3 hours, or if penetration is too shallow, the base is under-primed. Underpriming may be corrected by applying a second coating of the prime material.

An overprimed base may fail to cure and contribute to failure of the pavement. A free film of prime material remaining on the base after a 48-hour curing period indicates that the base is overprimed. This condition may be corrected by spreading a light, uniform layer of clean, dry sand over the prime coat to absorb the excess material. Application of the sand is usually followed by light rolling and brooming. Excess prime held in minor depressions should be corrected by an application of clean, dry sand. Any loose sand should be lightly broomed from the primed surface before the wearing surface is laid.

The primed base should be adequately cured before the wearing surface is laid. In general, a minimum of 48 hours should be allowed for complete curing. Ordinarily, proper surface condition is indicated by a slight change in the shiny black appearance to a slightly brown color.

When a soil base is to be covered by a bituminous wearing surface, the area should be barricaded to prevent traffic from carrying dust or mud onto the surface both before and after priming. If it is necessary to open the primed base course to traffic before it has completely cured, a fine sand may be used; and when ready to place the wearing surface, lightly broom the sand from the primed base course.

Single and Multiple Surface Treatments

A single surface treatment usually consists of a sprayed application of a bitumen and aggregate cover one stone thick. Surface treatment may be referred to as a seal coat, inverted penetration, armor coat, or carpet coat. A single surface treatment is usually less than 1/2 inch thick. Surface treatments serve as an abrasive and weather-resisting medium which waterproofs the base. Generally, they are not as durable as bituminous concrete and may require frequent maintenance. Surface treatments are particularly suitable for surfacing aged or worn bituminous pavements that are cracked, dry, reveled, or beginning to show signs of wear. When bituminous

pavements are designed and constructed properly, they should possess a surface texture that does not require surface treatment to fill the voids.

Surface treatments are used largely on roads, shoulders, and parking areas. Although not recommended for airstrips, they may be used as an expedient measure.

Surface treatments will not withstand the action of metal wheels on vehicles, tracked vehicles, or non-skid chains on vehicle wheels. Surface treatment should not be attempted except when the temperature is above 50°F. Three requirements for a surface treatment are:

1. The quantity of the bitumen must be sufficient to hold the stone without submerging it.
2. Sufficient aggregate must be used to cover the bitumen.
3. The base course on which the surface treatment is laid must be sufficiently strong to support the anticipated load.

A single surface treatment consists of an application of bitumen covered with mineral aggregate, rolled to provide a smooth, even-textured surface. Figure 5 shows the sequence of operations for the application of a single surface treatment.

Uniformly graded sand or crushed stone, gravel, or slag may be used for surface treatments. The purpose of the surface treatment determines the size of the aggregate to be selected. For example, coarse sand may be used for sealing a smooth existing surface. For a badly broken surface, the maximum size of the aggregate should be about 1/2 inch, and the mimimum size about 3/16 inch.

Rapid-cure cutbacks, medium-cure cutbacks, road tars, rapid-setting emulsions, and asphalt cements may be used for surface treatment. Rapid-cure cutbacks are most widely used because they evaporate rapidly and the road can be opened to traffic almost immediately after application of the surface treatment.

Surface treatments are usually applied to a thoroughly compacted primed base that has been swept clean. The existing surface or base course

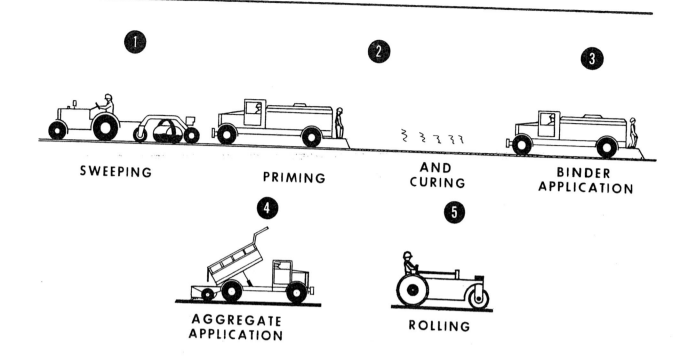

Figure 5.—Sequence of operations for the application of a single surface treatment.

must be dry, or contain moisture not in excess of that which will permit satisfactory bonding of surface treatment to the base. To assure uniform distribution, the bitumen should be applied with a bituminous distributor. The quantity of the bitumen required is based on the average particle size of the coverstone (aggregate). The bitumen must be sufficient to hold the aggregate in place without leaving a sticky surface. The aggregate must not be completely submerged in the bitumen. The viscosity used is dependent upon the size of the coverstone; the larger the coverstone, the higher (or thicker) the viscosity of the bitumen. One-quarter-inch aggregate should be submerged approximately 30 percent; 3/8-inch aggregate, 32 percent; 1/2-inch aggregate, 35 percent; and 3/4-inch aggregate, 43 percent. Approximately 1 gallon of bitumen is usually used for 100 pounds of aggregate.

The aggregate is spread immediately after application of the bitumen, while the bitumen is still fluid. An adjustable mechanical aggregate spreader may be used as shown in figure 6, or the aggregate may be spread from trucks or by hand. Trucks should be operated backwards so that the truck wheels will move over the bitumen that has been covered with aggregate.

For handspreading, aggregate should be dumped in piles adjacent to the areas to be treated.

During aggregate spreading, the surface is rolled with a 5- to 8-ton roller. A heavier roller is likely to crush the aggregate rather than embed the aggregate particles in the bitumen. Faulty rolling can be eliminated or minimized if the following practices are adhered to:

1. Rolling should be parallel to the centerline of the roadway to reduce the number of times the roller must change direction.
2. To assure complete coverage, succeeding passes should overlap one-half of the wheel width of the roller.
3. Rolling should be completed before the bitumen hardens. This will ensure that the aggregate becomes well embedded in the bitumen.
4. To maintain surface crown and to prevent feathering at the edges, succeeding passes should be made from the low side to the high side of the surface.
5. Rolling should be done at a slow speed.
6. Rolls should be wet to prevent bitumen from sticking to wheels.

11

Figure 6. — Hopper-type spreader applying aggregate to a surface treatment.

7. The power roll should pass over the unrolled surface before the steering roll.

After rolling and curing, the surface is ready for traffic. If the surface is used on an airfield, excess aggregate must be swept from the surface to avoid damage to aircraft. This practice is also recommended for roads, although it is not essential.

When a tougher, more resistant surface is desired than that obtained with a single surface treatment, multiple surface treatment may be used. Multiple surface treatment is two or more successive layers of a single surface treatment. Smaller particles of aggregate and correspondingly less bitumen are used for each successive layer. Although multiple surface treatments are usually more than 1 inch thick, they are still considered surface treatments because each layer is usually less than 1 inch and the total surface

treatment does not add appreciably to the load-carrying capacity of the base.

The first layer of a multiple surface treatment is laid in accordance with instructions given earlier for a single surface treatment.

Loose aggregate remaining on the first layer must be swept from the surface so that the layers may be bonded together. Remember that the size of the aggregate and the bitumen will decrease for each successive layer. For the second layer, the bitumen will usually be reduced one-third or one-half of the amount used in the first application. The aggregate used in the second application should be approximately one-half the diameter of that used in the first application. The final application is drag-broomed, if necessary, to provide an even layer of aggregate. At the time the surface is being drag-broomed, it should also be rolled with a 5- to 8-ton

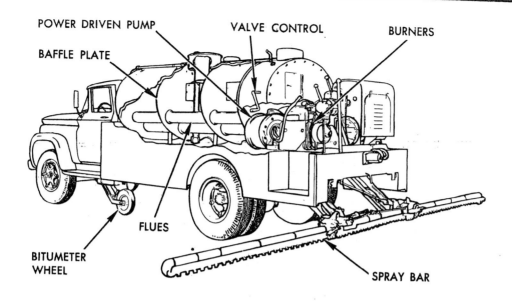

POWER DRIVEN PUMP   VALVE CONTROL   BURNERS

BAFFLE PLATE

FLUES

BITUMETER
WHEEL

SPRAY BAR

Figure   7. — Asphalt distributor.

roller so that the aggregate will become embedded in the bitumen. After the surface is
rolled and cured, it is ready for traffic. If
the multiple surface treatment has been laid
on an airfield, loose aggregate must be swept
from the surface so that it will not damage the
aircraft. Final sweeping is also recommended
for roads.

To prevent a soil wearing surface (dirt road)
from becoming excessively dusty, a bituminous
dust palliative (covering) is applied to hold
down the dust. The bituminous material used as
a dust palliative must be thin enough to soak
easily into the surface. It must also retain
fluidity indefinitely so that dust particles raised
by the traffic will become coated with the bituminous material. A medium-cure or slow-cure
cutback is the best material for this purpose.

ASPHALT DISTRIBUTOR

An asphalt distributor, illustrated in figure
7, is frequently used to spray bituminous
material on a prepared surface. The insulated
bitumen tank is equipped with heating flues for
application of heat from an oil burner. A gasoline
engine, mounted to the rear of the truck, provides power for an asphalt pump, fuel pump,
and air blower. The asphalt pump has an output
range from 30 to 350 gallons per minute. The

application rate of bitumen is controlled by the
width of the spray bar, pump output, and forward
speed of the truck after the bitumeter indicator
has been set. The spray bar width can vary
from 6 to 24 feet in width. The output of bitumen
will range from 1/10 to 3 gallons per square
yard. Where necessary, bituminous material
may be applied through an adjustable length
spray bar or a hand spray gun. The spray bar
may be of the circulating or noncirculating
type, depending upon the model of the distributor.
Flow of bituminous material is controlled by a
system of hand-operated valves. A tachometer
registers the pump discharge in gallons per
minute and/or speed of the engine, and a bitumeter shows the forward speed of the truck in
feet per minute. (See fig.   8.)

When applying asphalt for a prime or tack
coat, an over application of asphalt should be
avoided. For this reason, each distributor load
should be started out over building paper (sometimes called tar paper). This will also prevent
transverse overlap of material.

To maintain uniform pressure and temperature on all spray nozzles, the fan of the spray
from each nozzle must be uniform and set at
the proper angle with the spray bar (according
to the manufacturer's instructions) so that the
spray fans do not interfere with each other. The
spray bar must be maintained at the proper height

13

where the mix is dumped from a truck. A bar feeder on the hopper floor moves the mix to the spreading screws, which spread the mix in front of the screed unit. At the front of the screed assembly, a tamper bar strikes off the mat to the desired elevation and compacts it to as much as 85 percent of final density.

As shown in figure 10, the forward, beveled edge of the tamper does the compacting, while the lower edge does the striking off. Behind the tamper the screed slides along, giving the mat the final smooth finish.

A burner unit, figure 11, permits heating of the screed to prepare it for proper operating temperature. In general, the reason for heating the screed is to keep the asphalt material from sticking to it, and causing what is known as a drag to tear. Thickness of the mat is controlled by two thickness control screws as shown in figure 12. The screed may be adjusted at center to produce a crown. Normal width of the screed is 10 feet, but the width may be increased to 14 feet by use of screed extensions, or reduced to 8 feet by use of cutoff shoes. The finisher is usually powered by a gasoline engine, with a diesel engine being optional.

The manually operated dual controls of the model SA-35 finisher allow the operator to sit on the same side of the machine as the guideline or the edge of the existing mat (see fig. 13). This feature greatly eases longitudinal joint alignment control. Dual controls are most advantageous for paving in narrow places, such as parking areas and around airfield facilities. Operators may be stationed on both sides in such restricted places, greatly reducing the chance of collision and resulting damage to both the machine and objects nearby. Dual controls also allow operators to be trained in minimum time.

Assuming that the operations ahead of the paver have been properly performed, that the equipment is in good condition and properly adjusted, and that the paver is not placing the mix at an excessive rate of speed, there should be no need for hand work. Hand raking should not be done unless absolutely necessary. The most uniform surface texture can be obtained by keeping the hand work back of the paver to a minimum, except when it is required around obstacles.

Figure 8.—Bitumeter and tachometer dials.

above the road surface to provide complete and uniform overlap of the spray fans. The overlap can vary from 6 to 15 inches depending on the desired coverage and type of distributor used. The road speed must be uniform as determined by the type of surface treatment being applied.

ASPHALT FINISHER

While various makes and models of asphalt finishers are used in asphalt paving operations, the finisher most used for training and field operations is the Barber-Greene model SA-35 shown in figure 9.

When the surface has been cleaned, primed, and allowed to cure, it is ready for paving. In spreading mix, whether a hot or cold bituminous mixture, an asphalt finisher is used to lay the mixture into a smooth mat of required thickness and width. While the asphalt finisher shown in figure 16-9 is capable of handling up to 200 tons of mix per hour, its effective capacity is 100 tons per hour. The mat width may be varied from 8 to 14 feet, the depth from 1/2 to 6 inches, and the laydown speed from 12 to 64 feet per minute. The finisher consists essentially of a crawler-mounted tractor unit and a screed unit that is attached to the tractor. An 8-ton charging hopper is mounted on the front of the finisher

Figure 9. — Asphalt finisher.

On many jobs there are places where spreading with a paver is either impractical or impossible. In these cases, hand spreading is required. Placing and spreading by hand should be done very carefully and the material distributed uniformly so that segregation of the coarse aggregate and the bituminous binder will be avoided. If the asphalt mix is broadcast with shovels, almost complete segregation of the coarse and fine portions of the mix will result. The material should be deposited from the shovels into small piles which, in turn, are spread with LUTES or RAKES. In the spreading process, all material should be thoroughly loosened and evenly distributed. Any part of the mix that has formed into lumps and does not break down easily should be discarded. After the material has been placed, it is then rolled. In areas difficult to reach with a roller, hand tampers are used.

COMPACTION EQUIPMENT

The following discussion on compaction equipment is limited to that used in bituminous operations. Remember that the initial use of any compaction method should be on a trial-and-error basis.

Rollers used for compaction and final rolling of hot asphalt mix are the 10-ton three-wheel, two- and three-axle tandem, and multiple-wheel pneumatic rollers. Navy two-axle tandems usually weigh from 5 to 8 tons, and three-axle tandems

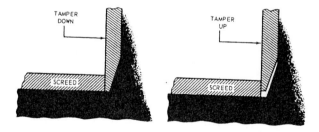

Figure 10. — Cross section of asphalt finisher tamper and screed.

15

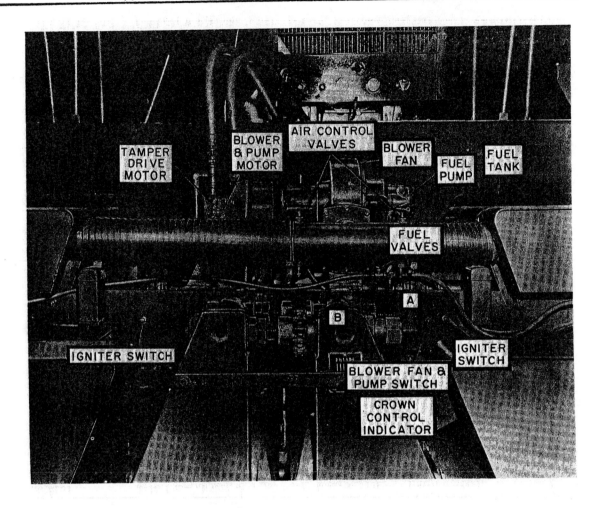

Figure 11. — Screed heater.

from 9 to 14 tons. Pneumatic tired rollers usually weigh 9 tons, fully ballasted.

Most compaction required in asphalt construction is achieved by the tamper on the finisher. Additional compaction and final surface texture are achieved by applying the rollers in the proper sequence. The hot mix should be at its optimum temperature for rolling when the rollers start to operate on the mat being laid. This optimum temperature will range between 225° to 250°F.

Breakdown rolling is done by the 10-ton three-wheel roller, secondary rolling by the two-axle tandem roller, and finish rolling by the penumatic-tired roller. With this combination of rollers, specified density should be obtained.

If the required density is not obtained during construction, subsequent traffic will further consolidate the asphalt surface and cause ruts.

Rolling of the longitudinal joint should be done immediately behind the finisher. The initial, or breakdown, pass with the roller should be made as soon as it is possible to roll the mixture without cracking the mat or having the mix pick up on the roller wheels. The second rolling should follow the breakdown rolling as closely as possible. The finish rolling should be done while the material is still workable enough for removal of roller marks. Generally speaking, longitudinal joint rolling should start directly behind the spreader; breakdown less than 200 feet behind the spreader; second rolling 200 feet or more behind the breakdown rolling; and

Figure 12. — Thickness control.

finish rolling as soon as possible behind the second rolling.

During rolling, the roller wheels should be kept moist, using only enough water to avoid picking up material. Rollers should move at a slow but uniform speed, with the drive rolls nearest the finisher. With the drive rolls moving toward the finisher, the material will have less tendency to be displaced, as shown in figure 14.

The line of rolling should not be suddenly changed or the direction of rolling suddenly

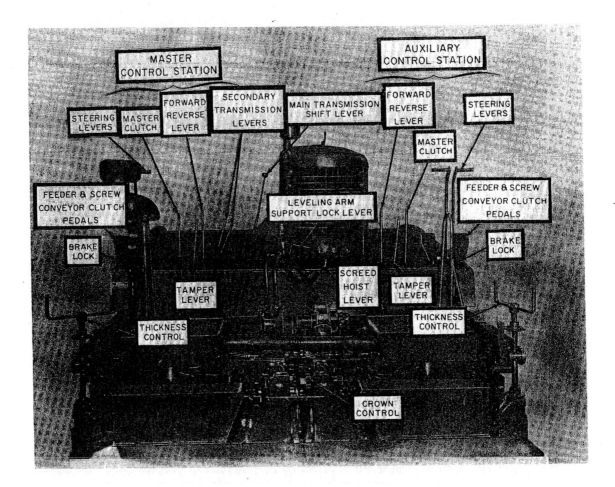

Figure 13.—Operating controls, Barber Greene model SA-35 finisher.

reversed, thereby displacing the mix. Any pronounced change in direction of the roller should be made on stable material. If the rolling causes displacement of the material, the affected areas should be loosened at once with rakes and restored to the original grade with loose material before being rerolled. Heavy equipment or rollers should not be permitted to stand on the finished surface until it has properly cooled or set. Rollers allowed to stand on a hot mat will sink in, thus causing depressions in the new mat.

When paving with a single finisher, the first lane placed should be rolled in the following order:

(1) Transverse joints.
(2) Outside edge.

(3) Breakdown rolling, beginning on the low side and working toward the high side.
(4) Second rolling, same procedure as (3).
(5) Finish rolling.

When paving with two finishers working in echelon, or abutting a previously placed lane, the mix should be rolled in the following order:

(1) Transverse joints.
(2) Longitudinal joints.
(3) Outside edge.
(4) Breakdown rolling.
(5) Second rolling.
(6) Finish rolling.

When paving in echelon, 6 to 8 inches of the edge which the second paver is following should

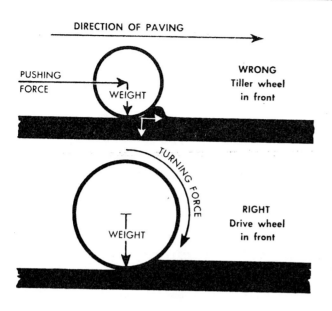

PUSHING FORCE

WEIGHT

WRONG
Tiller wheel
in front

TURNING FORCE

WEIGHT

RIGHT
Drive wheel
in front

Figure 14.—Rolling—direction is important.

be left unrolled. Then the second strip can be laid the same depth as the unrolled part of the first strip, and the roller can then compact the joint while the material is hot.

II. MAINTENANCE OF BITUMINOUS PAVEMENT

Maintenance and repair of roads and airfields are particularly important because of the constant and heavy mobility in modern warfare. Damage caused by the weight of heavy loads, by the abrasive action of military traffic, and by combat conditions must be repaired as quickly as possible. Repairs must often be made under difficulties, such as shortages of manpower, materials, and equipment; a lack of time; and the possibility of continuing or imminent attack.

Priority of maintenance and repair depends upon tactical requirements, traffic volume, and hazards that will result from complete failure of the paved area. A single pothole in a heavily used road, which is otherwise in excellent condition, should take priority over a pothole in an infrequently used road.

CAUSES OF SURFACE
FAILURE

The principal causes of surface failure are subgrade or base failure, disintegration of the surface, instability, or combat failure.

As you may know, an asphaltic concrete pavement is directly dependent upon its base for its load-carrying capacity. WHENEVER THE SUBGRADE OR BASE COURSE FAILS, THAT PART OF THE WEARING SURFACE IMMEDIATELY ABOVE THE WEAKENED AREA WILL ALSO FAIL. Factors which may cause a base to fail include inadequate drainage, frost action, poor compaction, improper materials used for the subgrade or base, and overloading by transporting of exceptionally heavy equipment and materials.

The disintegration, or decomposition, of a wearing surface may be the result of hardening of the bituminous film. This hardening process, usually referred to as oxidation, starts at the time the bitumen is applied and continues during the life of the wearing surface. Continuous exposure to the weather slowly hardens the bitumen, which loses its resiliency and becomes brittle. Hardening may be caused by poorly designed mix, incorrect proportioning of the aggregate and bitumen, or inadequate mixing.

Water may be responsible for surface failure by causing the asphalt film to separate from the surface of the aggregate. If the aggregate absorbs too much water, the aggregate and bitumen may separate.

An unstable wearing surface is likely to deform under the impact of traffic. Causes of instability are as follows:

1. Too much bitumen.
2. Smooth aggregate.
3. Bitumen that is too soft.
4. Low density resulting from insufficient compaction.
5. Unsuitable mix design or gradation of the aggregates, and unsatisfactory placement.
6. Uncured prime.
7. Overpriming or excessive tack coat.
8. Dirt between the surface and base course.

Continuous use of bituminous paved airfields by jet aircraft is likely to burn or scorch the surface, causing a pavement failure.

Other causes of surface failure are the use of unsuitable or insufficient bitumen, inadequate mixing, or a combination of these factors. The bitumen may also strip from dirty aggregate or be cut away by a petroleum distillate.

TYPES OF SURFACE FAILURE

Potholes are the most frequent type of failure found in bituminous wearing surfaces. Potholes may be caused by defective drainage, front action in the base, settlement of the base, or heavy traffic. A small pothole may be repaired with a hot or cold premix patch or a penetration patch. If a large area has many potholes, the entire area must be entirely reworked or replaced, depending upon the type of bituminous material used in the original pavement.

When the bond breaks down between the aggregate and bitumen a condition called raveling occurs. Raveling is disintegration of the surface, with damage starting at the top. This condition is frequently caused by a bitumen that becomes brittle and can no longer bind the aggregate together. A scorched bitumen or any of the factors that cause disintegration may produce reveling. Reveling is repaired by applying a skin patch or a seal coat (described later), as well as a fog seal or slurry seal.

Surface cracking first appears as minute hairline cracks visible only under careful scrutiny. The cracks run lengthwise of the road and appear to be numerous toward the edges of the traveled area. Surface water may seep through the cracks to the base and cause serious base failure and the formation of potholes. Cracks are cleaned with compressed air. Cracks wider than 1/8 inch are filled with lean sand-asphalt mix. The sand-asphalt mix is broomed into the cracks until they are full, then tamped with a spading tool. The filled cracks are sealed with asphalt and covered with sand. When surface cracks and checks are so extensive that water seeps through the cracks into the base course and endangers the pavement, a sand seal is applied. The pavement should be cleaned thoroughly and not more than 1/4 gallon per square yard of bituminous material applied. An even coating of clean, dry sand should be applied directly on the bitumen and rolled until the sand is well set. The area should not be opened to traffic until the bituminous seal has set and will not pick up under traffic.

Rutting and shoving of the wearing surface may be caused by instability. Defects caused by too much cutback in the bitumen may be corrected in road-mix pavement by blading the material from one side of the strip to the other until the volatile substances evaporate. For excess bitumen in the mix, sufficient new aggregate is added and mixing is continued until the bitumen is evenly distributed. The mix is then reshaped and rerolled, and a seal coat may be applied. In hot-mix pavements, excess bitumen requires removal and replacement of the affected area. Weakness of the base must be corrected by reworking the pavement.

Corrugation of a bituminous surface treatment frequently occurs when the bond has been broken between the surface and the underlying course. To repair this defect, the surface should be removed, the base reconditioned and primed, and a new surface treatment applied. Corrugation of a bituminous wearing surface may also be caused by any of the conditions discussed in the preceding paragraph and corrected in the same manner.

Bituminous materials that have been burned or overheated in processing of the mix become brittle and lifeless. The full depth of the pavement course constructed from such materials must be removed and replaced.

Bituminous surfaces frequently bleed, or exude bitumen, in hot weather. Bleeding causes a slippery condition that is hazardous to traffic and may possibly cause the surface to become rutted and grooved. This condition should be remedied as quickly as possible. Bleeding can be caused by too much bitumen being applied during prime coating or tack coating or by inadequate curing; in such cases the wearing surface must be replaced or reworked. As an expedient method for light bleeding, a light, uniform coat of fine aggregate or coarse sand should be applied. Fine sand is unsatisfactory. The pavement should be rolled, if possible, or the traffic permitted to compact the aggregate or sand. A light drag should be used to keep the aggregate or sand spread uniformly, and additional applications made as required. For heavy bleeding, a large aggregate is used.

When settlement is caused by failure of pipes, culverts, or supporting walls, repairs to these structures must be made before surfacing. Minor settlements and depressions frequently are repaired by surface treatments. The edge of a depression should be marked with chalk or paint.

The surface of the pavement within the marking should be cleaned thoroughly and a tack coat applied of not more than 0.1 gallon per square yard. Materials should be used similar in character and texture to those in the adjacent pavement. The patching material should be placed, raked, and rolled. Larger settled areas are repaired with one or more applications of bituminous material on top of the existing surface, or by removing the surface course and bringing the base up to proper grade. Under suitable weather conditions, many types of bituminous surfaces may be bladed to one side of the affected area and then relaid after the base is readjusted.

TYPES OF PATCHES

The types of patches used for repair of bituminous wearing surfaces are: premixed patch, penetration patch, skin patch, and seal coat (surface treatment). If damage is extensive, the entire paving system should be reworked or replaced.

Both hot and cold mixes are used for premixed bituminous patches. Small quantities of hot mix or cold mix often may be obtained locally or the mix may be prepared on the job. Hot mixes prepared at a central plant are generally used for extensive repair. Hot mix can be used with less delay from inclement weather than cold mix, and hot-mix patches can be opened to traffic in a shorter time. New cold-mix patches displace easily under traffic before the volatile substances have evaporated. Hot-mix patches have a longer life than cold-mix patches and less tendency to ravel at the edges. Hot-mix patching material is prepared in accordance with instructions set down at the central plant. In most cold-mixes, dry aggregate is required for a satisfactory mix. The amount of bitumen to be used is just as important in patching mixes as it is in mixes for construction of new pavements.

A penetration patch is made with macadam aggregate (which should be broken strone or slag, with a maximum size of 2 to 3 inches, depending on the depth of the hole) and a suitable bitumen.   Layers of suitable base material should be placed, compacted, lightly tacked, and a coarse layer of aggregate tamped into the hole which has been prepared in accordance with the procedures shown in figure   15. The bitumen used may be asphalt

cement or a rapid-curing emulsion. Rate of application is usually 1 gallon per square yard for the top inch, and 1/2 gallon per square yard for each additional inch of depth. Ensure that the final surface patched is slightly high to allow for compaction by traffic. Excess bituminous material should be avoided in a penetration patch. If time and personnel availability permit, a firm compaction of subbase material can be accomplished by repeatedly filling the pothole with materials on hand until the traffic has fully compacted the subbase. When traffic has sufficiently compacted the subbase, repair can proceed as illustrated in figure   15.

A skin patch is a single surface treatment used to correct cracking and raveling in small areas of the wearing surface. Skin patches seal the defective areas and recondition the wearing surface. In applying a skin patch, the damaged area is swept clean and a coat of asphalt cutback applied. The bituminous coat is then covered with fine aggregate and lightly rolled or tamped to seal the aggregate. The aggregate generally used is about 1/4-inch stone or clean, coarse sand. In general, approximately 1 gallon of bitumen is used for 100 pounds of aggregate, regardless of the size of the aggregate.

A seal coat is a single surface treatment used to seal large cracked or raveled areas. Basically, a seal coat is a sprayed application of bitumen covered with a thin layer of aggregate. The amount of bitumen depends upon the type of aggregate; usually about 1 gallon of bitumen is needed for every 100 pounds of aggregate. Double surface treatments may be used if necessary.

ASPHALT KETTLE

The asphalt kettle shown in figure 16 is equipped for hand-spraying bituminous materials for dressing stretches or road or runway shoulders, filling surface cracks, and spray coating areas for sheet asphalt repairs, surface treatment, or seal coating.

The trailer-mounted tank consists of an outer shell with a 165-gallon capacity storage and melting tank mounted inside. A removable fuel burner, mounted inside the kettle outer shell, provides heat to the melting tank through a baffle. A flue stack, located on the forward end of the melting tank over the top of the baffle and burner assembly, provides an escape for exhaust gases. A thermometer, inserted through

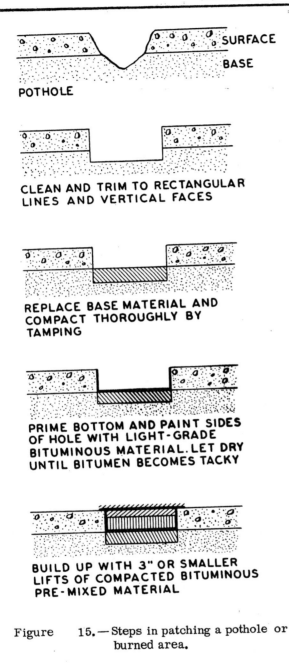

CLEAN AND TRIM TO RECTANGULAR
LINES AND VERTICAL FACES

REPLACE BASE MATERIAL AND
COMPACT THOROUGHLY BY
TAMPING

PRIME BOTTOM AND PAINT SIDES
OF HOLE WITH LIGHT-GRADE
BITUMINOUS MATERIAL. LET DRY
UNTIL BITUMEN BECOMES TACKY

BUILD UP WITH 3" OR SMALLER
LIFTS OF COMPACTED BITUMINOUS
PRE-MIXED MATERIAL

Figure 15.— Steps in patching a pothole or burned area.

an insulated pipe into the interior of the melting tank, indicates the temperature reading of the heating bituminous material. If the bituminous material is overheated, a fire or explosion can result.

A two-cylinder gasoline engine provides power for the bitumen pumping system. By shifting the clutch shifter lever, the engine is engaged

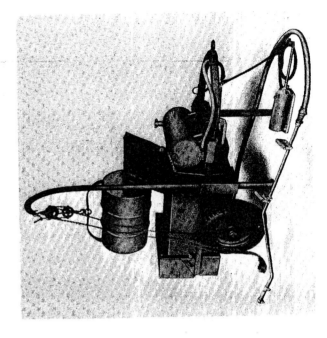

Figure 16.— Asphalt kettle.

to the pump assembly which provides the pressure for all pumping operations. A flexible, metal spray hose, which connects the pump to the hand-held spray bar assembly, is used to convey bitumen to the surface being repaired.

III. MAINTENANCE OF EQUIPMENT

As an Equipment Operator, it is your responsibility to coordinate the proper operation, care, use, adjusting, cleaning, preservation, and lubrication of paving and support equipment. This includes daily inspections and adjustments required for good operation. Malfunctions in equipment, which go beyond those operating adjustments performed by the EO, should be referred to the field mechanic for corrective action. This does not release you from working with the field mechanic unless directed otherwise.

You, the EO, serve a very important function in preventive maintenance. You are required to perform specific daily and scheduled maintenance services on your equipment. Proper performance of these services does much to prolong the life of the equipment, to avoid major repairs, and to assure that your equipment will perform its mission consistently and dependably. Acceptable maintenance standards applicable to any particular piece of equipment you operate have been established by the manufacturer of that equipment and should be followed. Instructions and directives put out by your unit must also be followed. They may include periodic inspections, testing, and observation of your operational techniques. You are responsible for certain forms, records, and reports in the performance of your maintenance services and daily operations. Get to know the applicable maintenance procedures and carry out the directives accordingly.

IV. PAVING SAFETY

This section deals with safety precautions applicable to paving operations. We are particularly interested in such topics as the heating of asphalt materials, traffic control, plant safety, equipment operation, cleaning bituminous handtools, and safe practices applicable to the personal safety of the operator and other persons who may be working as crewmembers.

Construction with bituminous materials involves several hazards. One of the most serious dangers is associated with the heating required to convert the solid or semi-solid materials to a degree of fluidity which will permit their application and/or mixing. As a safety measure, make sure fire extinguishing equipment (foamtype) is present at all times.

When readying the distributor and/or asphalt kettle, be sure they are in a level position before heating and are located a safe distance from buildings and other flammable materials. Keep covers closed during the heating period to prevent escape of flammable vapors, and avoid exposure to fumes from hot bituminous material — stay on the windward side.

When heating bituminous materials for spraying purposes, check the temperature suggested in table 2 for the type and grade being used. Remember that most of the flash points are exceeded before the materials reach spraying or working temperature; therefore, additional caution must be exercised to prevent the exposure of rising fumes to an open flame. A dense yellow cloud or vapor rising from the distributor or kettle is an indication that the material is being

Table 2. — Suggested Temperatures for Uses of Asphalt

Type and Grade of Asphalt	Pugmill Mixing Temperature of Aggregates*	Distributor Spraying Temperature
Asphalt Cements		
(For Open-Graded Mixes, Types I & II)**		
40-50	225-310°F	
60-70	225-305°F	
85-100	225-300°F	
120-150	225-300°F	
200-300	225-300°F	
(For Dense-Graded Mixes, Types III-VIII)**		
40-50	275-350°F	
60-70	265-330°F	
85-100	255-325°F	
120-150	245-325°F	
200-300	225-300°F	
(For Distributor Spray Applications)		
40-50***		300-410°F
60-70***		295-405°F
85-100		290-400°F
120-150		285-395°F
200-300		275-385°F
Liquid Asphalts		
RC, MC, and SC Grades		
30	60-105°F	
70	95-140°F	
250	135-175°F	
800	165-205°F	
3000	200-240°F	
Asphalt Emulsions		
RS-1	****	75-130°F
RS-2	****	110-160°F
MS-2	50-140°F	100-160°F
SS-1	50-140°F	75-130°F
SS-1h	50-140°F	75-130°F
RS-2K	****	75-130°F
RS-3K	****	110-160°F
CM-K	50-140°F	100-160°F
SM-K	50-140°F	100-160°F
SS-K	50-140°F	75-130°F
SS-Kh	50-140°F	75-130°F

*The temperature of the aggregates and asphalt immediately before mixing should be approximately that of the completed batch.
**Mix Type III is intermediate between dense- and open-graded mixes. As the gradation of the mix changes from dense-graded to open-graded the mixing temperature should be lowered accordingly.
***Not normally used for spray applications in pavement construction.
****Not used for mixing.

overheated to the extent that a small spark is sufficient to ignite the vapors.

Always extinguish burners before spraying bituminous material. When spraying, stand at least 25 feet clear of the spray bar on the bituminous distributor; spray bars have been known to blow open or rip with sudden pressure of heated materials. Remember that bituminous material must be heated to a high temperature, and any of this material coming in contact with the skin will leave a serious burn.

When handling asphalt being processed, wear proper protective apparel. Wear loose, heavy clothing—in good condition. Clothing should be closed at the neck, sleeves rolled down over the top of gloves, and trousers (without cuffs) extending well down over the top of shoes (safety type). Goggles should be worn to prevent eye burn from bubbling or splashing asphalt. In addition, wear a safety hat.

Frequently, bituminous operations will be planned for roads that must carry traffic while work is in progress. Slow signs or other warning devices should be conspicuously placed at both 100 yards and 20 yards from each entrance of the project. Flagmen, dressed in safety vests or some other attire, should aid in traffic control.

It will be necessary for most airfields to remain operational (if possible) during bituminous operations. The construction schedule, equipment routing, and maximum height of equipment should be discussed with the airfield safety officer. Liaison with air traffic control must be established if trucks and other equipment are to cross runways that are in use.

Guards, safety appliances, and similar devices are placed on moving parts in both asphalt and concrete plants for the protection of personnel. They must not be removed or made ineffective except for the purpose of making immediate repairs, lubrication, or adjustments, and then, only after the power has been shut off. All guards and devices must be replaced immediately after completion of repairs and adjustments by maintenance personnel.

There should be a platform near the truck loading or unloading area from which the mix or materials may be observed. There should also be a horn or buzzer for the plant operator to signal a truckdriver to move his vehicle. In addition, a "panic button," or switch, should be located a short distance from the plant. This panic button, or switch, can be used to stop all plant operations in event of an emergency. The area around mixing plants should be kept clean and clear of any waste material.

Machinery and mechanized equipment must be operated only by qualified and authorized personnel. It must not be operated in a manner that will endanger personnel or property, and the safe operating speeds or loads be exceeded. Equipment requiring an operator must not be permitted to run unattended. Mounting or dismounting equipment while in motion, or riding on equipment by unauthorized personnel, is prohibited. All equipment using fuel must be shut down, with ignition off, prior to and during refueling operations.

When operating paving equipment, frequent inspections of running mechanisms and attachments are the operator's responsibility. He is also responsible for inspecting such items as the power train, power plant, transmission, tracks, controls, skip guards, cables, sheaves, loading or unloading warning devices, and receiving hoppers.

In applying paving materials, crewmembers often become so occupied with their particular job that they are unaware of equipment operating near them. For this reason, at least one crewmember should be designated as safety inspector to ensure that reasonable precautions are observed within the assigned working areas. In addition, the safety inspector periodically holds short (approximately 5 to 15 minutes) safety meetings, called Stand-up Safety meetings, during which he briefs his crew on hazards and precautions relating to current work.

All handtools used for paving purposes must be kept in good repair and used only for the purpose for which designed. When using handtools such as rakes, shovels, lutes, and hand tampers on asphalt paving jobs, these tools should be heated before use and cleaned immediately after use. It is common practice to clean these handtools by burning off the bitumen collected during paving operations. Crewmembers should exercise caution and be forewarned that flames are not always visible. One man should stand by with a fire extinguisher capable of controlling a petroleum fire.

All personnel should be instructed to report promptly all personal injuries and property damage regardless of how minor. Reports should be prepared in accordance with instructions set forth in base of command publications.

V. CONCRETE TRANSIT MIXERS

The concrete transit mixer is a production tool designed to deliver and mix concrete. You, as an EO, are responsible for the safe and timely delivery of your load. You are also responsible

Figure 17.— Concrete transit mixer.

for manufacturing concrete and safeguarding the quality of the concrete en route to and at the jobsite until the concrete has been discharged.

OPERATING CONCRETE TRANSIT MIXERS

The information given below is on the Challenge series 01 concrete transit mixer (fig. 17), and applies ONLY to that machine. This information will give you an idea of how one of the several types of transit mixers is operated.

Before operating the transit mixer, you should first become familiar with its controls (fig. 18). The purpose of the various controls is explained below; the numbers in parentheses correspond to those used in figure 18 to indicate the location and purpose of the controls.

The CLUTCH LEVER (1) is known as the "Uni-Lever" in that the actions of the clutch, throttle, and drum rotation are incorporated in the one lever. The "Uni-Lever" located at the rear of the mixer has three functions. In addition to serving as clutch and throttle, the lever also controls the direction of drum rotation. The shifting of drum rotation may be accomplished ONLY at the rear station (2).

The HAND THROTTLE (3) is mounted on the auxiliary frame runner at the left front control station. The hand throttle is used (1)

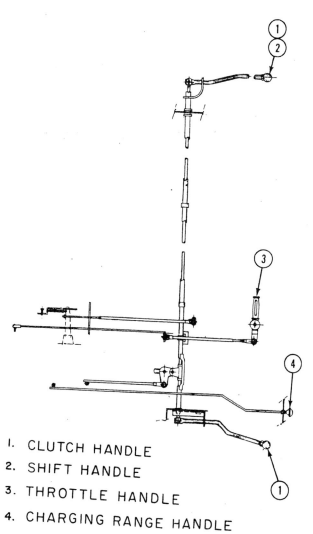

1. CLUTCH HANDLE
2. SHIFT HANDLE
3. THROTTLE HANDLE
4. CHARGING RANGE HANDLE

Figure 18.— Transit mixer controls.

to regulate engine speed while charging the mixer, (2) to set the engine speed for transit, and (3) for any other applications which may require a constant engine speed.

The CHARGING RANGE CONTROL LEVER (4) is located on the UPPER left corner of the instrument panel at the front control station. This lever is mechanically connected to the two-speed transmission; this gives the operator an additional speed range for charging. To select the desired speed range, disengage the clutch, select the appropriate speed range, and re-engage the clutch.

Before you can fulfill your responsibility as a transit truck mixer operator, some basic knowledge of the nature of concrete and of its proper mixing procedures must be known.

The basic ingredients of concrete are aggregates (such as gravel and crushed stone), sand, cement, and water. Small quantities of admixtures may also be added to achieve certain characteristics such as air entrainment or better workability. The aggregates normally comprise approximately 65 to 80 percent of the total volume of ingredients, while the cement and water together comprise about 20 to 35 percent.

Various kinds of concrete are produced to meet specific needs in construction work. Concrete of the desired quality is obtained by varying the sizes, types, and quantities of aggregates, as well as the type and amount of cement, the amount of water, and the types and amounts of admixtures. The kinds and quantities of each material are spelled out in a "mix design" for specific jobs and are standardized for many jobs that are similar in nature.

Types of Mixer Operation

The transit truck mixer is used with any type of ready mix concrete mixing and hauling procedure, including central mixing, shrink mixing, transit mixing and jobsite mixing. In hauling central mixed concrete the truck mixer serves as an agitator keeping the concrete well mixed en route to the job by turning the drum at agitating speed. In shrink mix operations the materials are combined and the mixing process is begun at the plant. Then the concrete is loaded into the mixer, and the mixing is completed in the truck mixer. In transit mixing the materials are loaded into the truck mixer at the plant, and all of the mixing is accomplished by the truck mixer en route to the job. Some project plans specify that the concrete must be mixed at the jobsite. On this type of operation, all the materials except the water are loaded into the truck mixer drum at the plant. The mixer, equipped with one of the optional large water tanks and water measuring devices, adds the mixing water at the jobsite and performs the entire mixing operation there.

Ideal Mixing Conditions

Ideal conditions for mixing concrete include simultaneous loading of cement, sand, water and aggregate (to obtain initial intermingling of materials), followed by 70 to 100 turns of the mixer drum at normal mixing speeds of approximately 7 to 11 rpm. Of these three critical steps: proper charging, adequate drum speed, and the correct number of drum revolutions during the mixing cycle, the charging operation (described later in this chapter) is most important.

At variations from simultaneous loading will make mixing more difficult and will require additional drum revolutions at mixing speed.

Avoid Overmixing

Overmixing damages the quality of the concrete, tends to grind the aggregates into smaller pieces, increases the temperature of the mixture, lowers the slump, decreases air entrainment, and decreases the strength of the concrete. Overmixing also puts NEEDLES WEAR on the drum and blades.

In selecting the best mixing speed for each trip, the operator of a transit mixer should estimate the travel time (in minutes) to the job and divide this into the minimum desired number of revolutions at mixing speed—70. The result will be the best drum speed. For instance, if the haul is 10 minutes, 70 divided by 10 equals 7. With this drum speed, the load will arrive on the job with exactly 70 turns at mixing speed—no overmixing and no unnecessary equipment wear. If the load cannot be discharged immediately, the driver should turn it at 2 rpm (minimum agitating speed) until he can discharge it. Since he arrived on the job with no more than the minimum number of mixing turns completed, he is able to wait longer (if necessary) without accumulating more than the maximum permissible number of total turns (250).

To simplify the selection of proper mixing speeds and to allow a margin for error that will cover variations in driving conditions, the operator may choose to use mixing speeds between 5 and 10 rpm, rather than 4 to 12 rpm. Working within the 5 to 10 rpm range, dividing 70 by estimated travel time will produce the desired drum speed for any trip from 7 to 14 minutes in length. For trips shorter than 7 minutes, the driver will continue to turn his drum at 10 rpm for the full 7 minutes, even though a portion of that time is at the jobsite. For trips longer than 14 minutes in length, the driver will maintain a drum speed of 5 rpm for 14 minutes (producing a total of 70 turns at mixing speed), then change to 2 rpm (agitating speed) for the balance of the trip, and for waiting time on the job, if any.

Batching and Charging Procedures

In order to produce quality concrete, you should strive to obtain uniform ribbon loading of all materials throughout the entire charging operation. Ribbon loading is best because it allows intermingling of the materials as they enter the drum, providing a head start on the mixing operations.

For transit mixing and jobsite mixing, the mixer should be charged with the truck engine running at near full throttle and the mixer control lever in the charge position. This will produce a drum speed of about 16 rpm. For central mix and shrink mix operations a little less throttle, which will produce a charge speed of 12 to 14 rpm, is generally adequate. As soon as the load is charged, the hand throttle or remote throttle should be closed and the drum speed reduced to the desired mixing speed.

Discharging

The unloading operation can be controlled from the control station at the rear or from the cab, whichever seems to best suit the job conditions. In either case, the throttle should be set partially open and the discharge speed controlled with the mixer control lever. Returning the control lever to its neutral position will automatically stop the drum. If the interruption is of any significant length, the control lever should be moved to agitate speed. The load can also be discharged with the truck in motion if required, such as in curb and gutter placement. With the mixer engine throttle positioned for slow speed, the "Uni-Lever" can be moved to whatever position will produce the needed discharge rate to fill the forms.

When discharging concrete from a mixer equipped with a sealing door, the door should be opened wide to prevent segregation or straining of materials. When discharging is intermittent as in wheelbarrows, buggies, buckets, etc., the rate should be controlled by manipulation of the mixer control lever — not the engine throttle.

Mixer Cleaning

At the jobsite: Immediately after discharging all concrete to the required project, you should wash off the excess concrete in the mixer drum and blades, the discharge opening, and the discharge chutes before it has a chance to harden. Spraying 15 to 25 gallons of water into the drum while it is revolving will clean the inside of the drum as well as remove all grout which may have collected in the water nozzle during discharge. This may be carried back to the plant and subtracted from the next load. A wash-down hose is provided to clean areas accessible from the outside. A clean mixer produces a more satisfactory mixing and discharging of concrete.

> CAUTION: Wash the mixer with water only for the first 30 days of operation. Any stains occurring within the first 30 days can be washed off with a mild detergent. Thoroughly rinse with clear water. Avoid washing in the sun. The use of acids or abrasives may cause severe loss of gloss.

At the plant: A minimum of 150 to 250 gallons of water, depending on the size of the mixer, should be used to thoroughly clean the drum immediately at the end of each day's run. With the flush water in the drum, rotate the drum in the mixing direction for a few minutes, then discharge the flush water at maximum drum rpm. Complete cleaning the outside of the mixer, particularly around the discharge end.

By using a mixture of half paraffin oil and half diesel oil, the truck and concrete mixer can be sprayed in a few minutes; this prevents or retards the concrete from adhering to the structural members. After the entire unit has been thoroughly sprayed, it can be washed down with an ordinary garden hose at the prescribed line pressure.

If the above procedure is followed daily, it will result in increased efficiency, as well as reduce maintenance costs, of the equipment.

Hydraulic Chute Hoist

The manual hydraulic chute hoist is simple to operate and requires very little maintenance.

This hoist consists of an oil reservoir and a hydraulic pump with a flow control valve and a hydraulic cylinder secured to the chute. By hand pumping and manipulation of the flow control valve, the operator may raise, hold, or lower the chute to any desired position.

Hints for trouble free operation:

1. Check oil level in reservoir.
2. Keep breather on top of reservoir clean. If this breather becomes clogged, a vacuum will result.
3. Use clean oil when adding oil.

The friction lock chute brake is designed to control the swing of the chute through a 180° range. The operator may lock it at any position simply by tightening down on the handle, or it may be desirable to apply just enough drag so that a slight tug will move the chute. This arrangement may save damage to the chute in case it is forced against a solid object.

SECURING

When securing a concrete transit mixer, position the concrete discharge chute so that it is parallel to the mixer drum. Wash down the unit as described in previous paragraphs, place mixer controls in neutral, and secure mixer engine. Drive the transit truck to the designated securing area and position in a safe manner.

VI. OPERATOR'S CARE AND MAINTENANCE

Every operator is required to perform certain daily maintenance services on the concrete transit mixer he operates. This maintenance includes the required inspection service, lubrication, and adjustments required to maintain the concrete transit mixer in a safe and operable condition, prevent malfunctions, and avoid or delay major repairs.

In order to maintain efficient operation of the mixer, it is important that you clean the mixer thoroughly once a day, in addition to washing it down after discharging each load. Lubricate the mixer and the mixer engine daily, in accordance with the manufacturer's instructions. Service the engine air filter regularly, check the

truck frame and mixer mounting bolts, and maintain correct drum chain adjustment.

Oils which are used in the hydraulic system perform the dual function of lubrication and transmission of power. Select and use only the type recommended by the manufacturer.

Special worm gear or compound steam cylinder oil is used in the worm gear drive. Do not use automotive or hypoid type "all purpose" oil. Do not add any compound. Check oil level daily, change oil after 2 weeks of operation and every 3 months thereafter. The oil capacity is given on the instruction plate attached to the mixer housing.

The frequency of oil change and oil filter element replacement for the mixer engine depends upon the operating conditions encountered. Under normal operating conditions, the oil and filter element should be changed after every 100 hours of operation.

Since engines used in mixers may vary, it is advisable that you comply with the recommended oil viscosity, general care, and maintenance procedures outlined in the manufacturer's operating manual.

The lubricant used on the mixer roller chain must be thin enough to enter a chain joint and must be applied frequently enough that a film of lubrication is constantly maintained inside the joints. A coating of hard grease will collect and hold abrasive particles, resulting in undue wear on both chains and sprockets. To prevent corrosion, reduce wear rate of chains, and lengthen sprocket life, use of SAE 30 engine oil is recommended by the manufacturer for mixer chain lubrication. Apply oil to the chain joints daily with an oil can or brush.

VII. TRANSIT MIXER SAFETY

The increased use of transit mix trucks on construction projects imposes traffic problems which must be considered. Caution must be used during backing of the transit truck. Backing should be controlled by a signalman, positioned so that the operator can clearly observe the directions given.

Use extreme caution when traveling over uneven terrain on a construction site. The stability of the mixer is greatly reduced with the extra weight of the concrete in the mixer unit. In such cases, a slow speed is recommended.

Some additional safety precautions that must be observed are as follows:

1. Reduce speed before making a turn or applying the truck brakes.

2. Secure discharge chute properly, using the friction brake lock provided.

3. Check to make certain that other personnel are in the clear before starting the mixer charging or discharging.

4. Before making any adjustments, make certain that the mixer engine is not running; this is particularly important when the clutch or drum chain is to be adjusted.

5. Secure mixer engine before refueling.

ANSWER SHEET

T NO. _____ PART _____ TITLE OF POSITION _____

(AS GIVEN IN EXAMINATION ANNOUNCEMENT - INCLUDE OPTION, IF ANY)

CE OF EXAMINATION _____ DATE _____

(CITY OR TOWN)   (STATE)

RATING

USE THE SPECIAL PENCIL.   MAKE GLOSSY BLACK MARKS.

	A B C D E		A B C D E		A B C D E		A B C D E		A B C D E
1	⦂⦂⦂⦂⦂	26	⦂⦂⦂⦂⦂	51	⦂⦂⦂⦂⦂	76	⦂⦂⦂⦂⦂	101	⦂⦂⦂⦂⦂
2	⦂⦂⦂⦂⦂	27	⦂⦂⦂⦂⦂	52	⦂⦂⦂⦂⦂	77	⦂⦂⦂⦂⦂	102	⦂⦂⦂⦂⦂
3	⦂⦂⦂⦂⦂	28	⦂⦂⦂⦂⦂	53	⦂⦂⦂⦂⦂	78	⦂⦂⦂⦂⦂	103	⦂⦂⦂⦂⦂
4	⦂⦂⦂⦂⦂	29	⦂⦂⦂⦂⦂	54	⦂⦂⦂⦂⦂	79	⦂⦂⦂⦂⦂	104	⦂⦂⦂⦂⦂
5	⦂⦂⦂⦂⦂	30	⦂⦂⦂⦂⦂	55	⦂⦂⦂⦂⦂	80	⦂⦂⦂⦂⦂	105	⦂⦂⦂⦂⦂
6	⦂⦂⦂⦂⦂	31	⦂⦂⦂⦂⦂	56	⦂⦂⦂⦂⦂	81	⦂⦂⦂⦂⦂	106	⦂⦂⦂⦂⦂
7	⦂⦂⦂⦂⦂	32	⦂⦂⦂⦂⦂	57	⦂⦂⦂⦂⦂	82	⦂⦂⦂⦂⦂	107	⦂⦂⦂⦂⦂
8	⦂⦂⦂⦂⦂	33	⦂⦂⦂⦂⦂	58	⦂⦂⦂⦂⦂	83	⦂⦂⦂⦂⦂	108	⦂⦂⦂⦂⦂
9	⦂⦂⦂⦂⦂	34	⦂⦂⦂⦂⦂	59	⦂⦂⦂⦂⦂	84	⦂⦂⦂⦂⦂	109	⦂⦂⦂⦂⦂
10	⦂⦂⦂⦂⦂	35	⦂⦂⦂⦂⦂	60	⦂⦂⦂⦂⦂	85	⦂⦂⦂⦂⦂	110	⦂⦂⦂⦂⦂

Make only ONE mark for each answer.   Additional and stray marks may be
counted as mistakes.   In making corrections, erase errors COMPLETELY.

	A B C D E		A B C D E		A B C D E		A B C D E		A B C D E
11	⦂⦂⦂⦂⦂	36	⦂⦂⦂⦂⦂	61	⦂⦂⦂⦂⦂	86	⦂⦂⦂⦂⦂	111	⦂⦂⦂⦂⦂
12	⦂⦂⦂⦂⦂	37	⦂⦂⦂⦂⦂	62	⦂⦂⦂⦂⦂	87	⦂⦂⦂⦂⦂	112	⦂⦂⦂⦂⦂
13	⦂⦂⦂⦂⦂	38	⦂⦂⦂⦂⦂	63	⦂⦂⦂⦂⦂	88	⦂⦂⦂⦂⦂	113	⦂⦂⦂⦂⦂
14	⦂⦂⦂⦂⦂	39	⦂⦂⦂⦂⦂	64	⦂⦂⦂⦂⦂	89	⦂⦂⦂⦂⦂	114	⦂⦂⦂⦂⦂
15	⦂⦂⦂⦂⦂	40	⦂⦂⦂⦂⦂	65	⦂⦂⦂⦂⦂	90	⦂⦂⦂⦂⦂	115	⦂⦂⦂⦂⦂
16	⦂⦂⦂⦂⦂	41	⦂⦂⦂⦂⦂	66	⦂⦂⦂⦂⦂	91	⦂⦂⦂⦂⦂	116	⦂⦂⦂⦂⦂
17	⦂⦂⦂⦂⦂	42	⦂⦂⦂⦂⦂	67	⦂⦂⦂⦂⦂	92	⦂⦂⦂⦂⦂	117	⦂⦂⦂⦂⦂
18	⦂⦂⦂⦂⦂	43	⦂⦂⦂⦂⦂	68	⦂⦂⦂⦂⦂	93	⦂⦂⦂⦂⦂	118	⦂⦂⦂⦂⦂
19	⦂⦂⦂⦂⦂	44	⦂⦂⦂⦂⦂	69	⦂⦂⦂⦂⦂	94	⦂⦂⦂⦂⦂	119	⦂⦂⦂⦂⦂
20	⦂⦂⦂⦂⦂	45	⦂⦂⦂⦂⦂	70	⦂⦂⦂⦂⦂	95	⦂⦂⦂⦂⦂	120	⦂⦂⦂⦂⦂
21	⦂⦂⦂⦂⦂	46	⦂⦂⦂⦂⦂	71	⦂⦂⦂⦂⦂	96	⦂⦂⦂⦂⦂	121	⦂⦂⦂⦂⦂
22	⦂⦂⦂⦂⦂	47	⦂⦂⦂⦂⦂	72	⦂⦂⦂⦂⦂	97	⦂⦂⦂⦂⦂	122	⦂⦂⦂⦂⦂
23	⦂⦂⦂⦂⦂	48	⦂⦂⦂⦂⦂	73	⦂⦂⦂⦂⦂	98	⦂⦂⦂⦂⦂	123	⦂⦂⦂⦂⦂
24	⦂⦂⦂⦂⦂	49	⦂⦂⦂⦂⦂	74	⦂⦂⦂⦂⦂	99	⦂⦂⦂⦂⦂	124	⦂⦂⦂⦂⦂
25	⦂⦂⦂⦂⦂	50	⦂⦂⦂⦂⦂	75	⦂⦂⦂⦂⦂	100	⦂⦂⦂⦂⦂	125	⦂⦂⦂⦂⦂

ANSWER SHEET

TEST NO. ____________ PART ______ TITLE OF POSITION ____________________
(AS GIVEN IN EXAMINATION ANNOUNCEMENT - INCLUDE OPTION, IF ANY)

PLACE OF EXAMINATION ____________________ (CITY OR TOWN) ____________ (STATE) DATE ________

RATING

USE THE SPECIAL PENCIL. MAKE GLOSSY BLACK MARKS.

1 A B C D E	26 A B C D E	51 A B C D E	76 A B C D E	101 A B C D E
2 A B C D E	27 A B C D E	52 A B C D E	77 A B C D E	102 A B C D E
3 A B C D E	28 A B C D E	53 A B C D E	78 A B C D E	103 A B C D E
4 A B C D E	29 A B C D E	54 A B C D E	79 A B C D E	104 A B C D E
5 A B C D E	30 A B C D E	55 A B C D E	80 A B C D E	105 A B C D E
6 A B C D E	31 A B C D E	56 A B C D E	81 A B C D E	106 A B C D E
7 A B C D E	32 A B C D E	57 A B C D E	82 A B C D E	107 A B C D E
8 A B C D E	33 A B C D E	58 A B C D E	83 A B C D E	108 A B C D E
9 A B C D E	34 A B C D E	59 A B C D E	84 A B C D E	109 A B C D E
10 A B C D E	35 A B C D E	60 A B C D E	85 A B C D E	110 A B C D E

Make only ONE mark for each answer. Additional and stray marks may be counted as mistakes. In making corrections, erase errors COMPLETELY.

11 A B C D E	36 A B C D E	61 A B C D E	86 A B C D E	111 A B C D E
12 A B C D E	37 A B C D E	62 A B C D E	87 A B C D E	112 A B C D E
13 A B C D E	38 A B C D E	63 A B C D E	88 A B C D E	113 A B C D E
14 A B C D E	39 A B C D E	64 A B C D E	89 A B C D E	114 A B C D E
15 A B C D E	40 A B C D E	65 A B C D E	90 A B C D E	115 A B C D E
16 A B C D E	41 A B C D E	66 A B C D E	91 A B C D E	116 A B C D E
17 A B C D E	42 A B C D E	67 A B C D E	92 A B C D E	117 A B C D E
18 A B C D E	43 A B C D E	68 A B C D E	93 A B C D E	118 A B C D E
19 A B C D E	44 A B C D E	69 A B C D E	94 A B C D E	119 A B C D E
20 A B C D E	45 A B C D E	70 A B C D E	95 A B C D E	120 A B C D E
21 A B C D E	46 A B C D E	71 A B C D E	96 A B C D E	121 A B C D E
22 A B C D E	47 A B C D E	72 A B C D E	97 A B C D E	122 A B C D E
23 A B C D E	48 A B C D E	73 A B C D E	98 A B C D E	123 A B C D E
24 A B C D E	49 A B C D E	74 A B C D E	99 A B C D E	124 A B C D E
25 A B C D E	50 A B C D E	75 A B C D E	100 A B C D E	125 A B C D E